D0577408

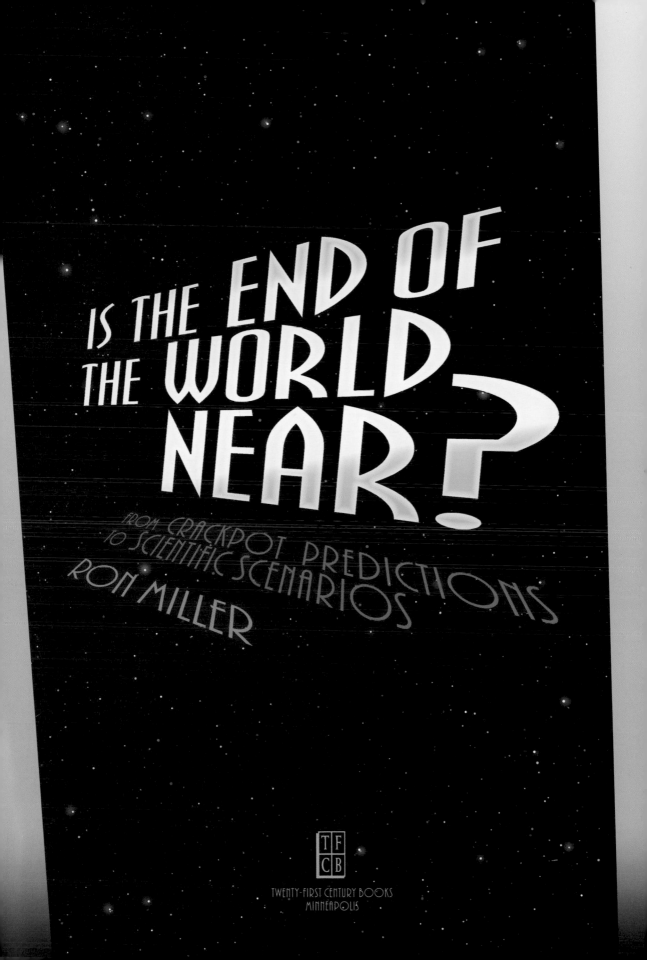

IS THE END OF THE WORLD NEAR?

FROM CRACKPOT PREDICTIONS TO SCIENTIFIC SCENARIOS

RON MILLER

TFCB

TWENTY-FIRST CENTURY BOOKS
MINNEAPOLIS

FOR NOAH AND SOMMER, WHOSE LOVE WILL SURELY OUTLAST EVEN CHAPTER 8
—R.M.

Twenty-First Century Books
A division of Lerner Publishing Group, Inc.
241 First Avenue North
Minneapolis, MN 55401 U.S.A.

Website address: www.lernerbooks.com

Main body text set in Barcelona ITG Std.—Book 11/16.
Typeface provided by International Typeface Corp.

Library of Congress Cataloging-in-Publication Data

Miller, Ron, 1947–
Is the end of the world near? : from crackpot predictions to
scientific scenarios / by Ron Miller.
p.   cm.
Includes bibliographical references and index.
ISBN 978-0-7613-7396-4 (lib. bdg. : alk. paper)
1. End of the world (Astronomy) 2. Science—Miscellanea. I. Title.
QB638.8.M55 2012
2010051963
001.9—dc22

Manufactured in the United States of America
1 – MG – 7/15/11

CONTENTS

This is Earth. We live, work, and play here. But how long will our planet last? Read on to find out.

INTRODUCTION

At one time or another, just about everyone has used the phrase "the end of the world." For most, this simply refers to a big disappointment. For instance, it would be "the end of the world" for some people if they didn't get a date for the prom or if their Twitter account were suddenly disconnected.

For others, "the end of the world" means the end of complex human society. They envision a world in which human government and social systems have broken down—a world without electricity, science, or long-distance communication, a world in which buildings, machines, and roads have fallen into disrepair.

Other end-of-the-world scenarios include the end of human life or the end of life of any kind. People also wonder about the destruction of Earth itself and the demise of the Sun, the solar system, and even the entire universe. People have studied, worried, and warned about all these scenarios for thousands of years.

THE END IS NEAR?

The end of the world has fascinated and frightened humankind for tens of thousands of years. Many people have made specific predictions about the end of the world, including when and how it will happen. Some of these predictions have had a scientific basis—or at least one that seemed scientific. Other predictions have been based on religious beliefs. For instance, Christian prophets have been predicting the end of the world for centuries.

One of the most recent end-of-the-world predictions centers on the date December 21, 2012. People have produced dozens of books, movies, and television shows about how and why the world will end on that day. If you do an Internet search for "December 21, 2012," you'll get millions of results. If you're reading this book after December 21, 2012, you'll know that the prediction didn't pan out.

CERTAINTIES AND UNCERTAINTIES

Is the world going to come to an end? The simple answer is yes. Scientists know that more than one billion years from now, the Sun will become much brighter and hotter. The heat will evaporate, or dry up, all the water on Earth. Nothing—including people—will be able to live on the hot, dry planet. It will become a stark, lifeless desert. Billions of years after that, the Sun will grow to an enormous size. It will burn up nearby planets and turn Earth into a ball of melted rock. Eventually, the Sun will run out of fuel and die. Earth and other planets will become cold, dark cinders.

But long before any of that happens, the world—or human life as we know it—might end in any number of ways. People might bring about their own destruction, or natural forces might destroy Earth and all its inhabitants. In this book, we'll examine end-of-the-world scenarios—from the fantastic to the truly terrifying. We'll find out which predictions to shrug off and which ones to really worry about.

An intersection in New York City, one of the world's busiest cities, teems with people, cars, and cabs. In the early twenty-first century, almost seven billion people lived on planet Earth. What does the future hold for Earth and its inhabitants?

In this eighteenth-century illustration, the Norse god Heimdal blows his horn before the epic battle at Ragnarok. Most of the world's cultures have beliefs and myths about how the world will one day end.

CHAPTER 1
FANTASY, FAITH, AND FICTION

People have been predicting the end of the world since ancient times. One example comes from the ancient Norse people. They inhabited modern-day Scandinavia (Norway, Sweden, and Denmark) from about 3000 B.C. to about A.D. 1000. According to Norse mythology, sometime in the future, the Norse gods and their enemies would have a big battle called Ragnarok. One by one, the gods would fall in battle. When the last one died, the Sun, the Moon, Earth, and everyone living on Earth would die too.

The Sioux people are a Native American group. They have lived on the northern Great Plains, in what is now the United States, for thousands of years. The Sioux end-of-the-world story involves an extremely old woman who lives in a hidden cave. According to the story, she has lived in the cave for one thousand years. All that time, she has been making a decoration for her buffalo robe. The decoration is made of porcupine quills, which are dyed in beautiful colors. The old woman works by a fire, which she has kept going for the entire thousand years. She cooks a delicious berry soup over the fire. Every now and then, she gets up to stir the soup. Every time she does, her big black dog pulls some of the quills from her buffalo robe decoration.

ESCHATOLOGY

The study of the ways in which the world might end is called eschatology. The term comes from *eschatos* and *logia*, Greek words meaning "last" and "study of." Eschatologists primarily concern themselves with the end of the world as depicted in religion, myth, and philosophy.

FANTASY, FAITH, AND FICTION

9

So she never finishes her work. The Sioux people say that if she ever finishes the decoration, the world will come to an end.

MODERN WORLD RELIGIONS AND THE END OF THE WORLD

The world's major religions all have stories about the end of the world. An example comes from Hinduism. This religion developed in India more than three thousand years ago. In modern times, millions of people practice the Hindu faith. Hinduism tells how someday humanity will descend into a dark age. It will be a time of violence, disease, and moral decay. Then the Hindu god Vishnu will come to Earth in the form of a figure called Kalki. He will ride a white horse and carry a sword. Kalki will destroy all evil on Earth. The existing world will end, but a new Golden Age will begin.

Buddhism is another major modern religion. Founded in India in about 500 B.C., it is based on the teachings of Siddhartha Gautama, a holy man known as the Buddha. In a story called the Sermon of the Seven Suns, Buddha tells how the world will end. First, Earth will suffer from drought—a long period of no rainfall. All the plants will wither and die. Then, many years later, a second Sun will appear in the sky. This Sun will dry up all the brooks and

In the Hindu end-of-the-world story, Vishnu, riding a white horse, rids the world of evil and disease.

ponds on Earth. Then a third Sun will appear and dry up all the big rivers. A fourth Sun will dry up all the big lakes. A fifth Sun will dry up the oceans. With the appearance of the sixth Sun, volcanoes will erupt all around Earth. Finally, with the seventh Sun, Earth will become a great ball of fire.

Christianity is based on the life and teachings of a man named Jesus. He lived in the Middle East in the first century A.D. Christians believe that Jesus is the son of God. Christian teaching is put forth in a book called the Bible. According to the Book of Revelation, part of the New Testament (the second section of the Christian Bible), a great battle between God and Satan (the devil) will occur at a place called Armageddon. After the triumph of God, according to the story, Earth and heaven will be destroyed—an event called the Apocalypse. The Book of Revelation also says that the Apocalypse will be the Day of Judgment. On this day, God will separate religious believers from nonbelievers. After this judgment, nonbelievers will be destroyed along with Earth. Believers will be transported to an ideal world and will have eternal life.

WAITING FOR THE APOCALYPSE

The Book of Revelation says that Judgment Day will come after a one-thousand-year period. The book was written around A.D. 95, but most early Christians started the one-thousand-year count from the year 1. So they thought the thousand years would be up in A.D. 1000. When that year approached, Christians braced themselves for Judgment Day. But the Earth did not end when the year 1000 arrived.

Many Christians still await Judgment Day, or the "end times." This name for the Apocalypse comes from the Book of Daniel, another part of the Bible. Some people who studied this book determined that the end of the world would come on May 21, 2011, but that prediction didn't prove correct either.

Many Christians view terrorism, disease, and economic crises as signs that the end of the world is near. The Book of Revelation says that a ferocious global war will take place before Judgment Day. Some modern believers have armed themselves in preparation for this war. Others do not fear the war, which they believe will hasten the Apocalypse. They have faith that as devout Christians, they will survive the fighting and end up in an ideal world with God.

This scene on the Bayeux Tapestry (woven in eleventh-century France) shows Halley's comet, visible from Earth in 1066, streaking through the sky. In earlier centuries, some people feared that comets and other space phenomena signaled the end of the world.

FALSE ALARMS

In earlier centuries, people didn't understand the workings of the Sun, Earth, the Moon, and other objects in space. When unusual events happened in space, some people feared that the end of the world was near. For instance, during a solar eclipse, the Moon passes between the Sun and Earth. The Moon blocks the Sun's light. For a time during a solar eclipse, the sky can grow completely dark in daytime. In earlier eras, people didn't understand eclipses or why they darkened the sky. Some people thought the Sun would disappear forever and the world would end during an eclipse. People in earlier eras also worried that passing comets would bring about the end of the world. In 1910, when Halley's comet passed near Earth, some people panicked. They thought that gases in the comet's tail would poison people on Earth.

In reality, unless they actually slam into Earth, passing comets pose no danger. And eclipses do no harm to the Sun or Earth, but they can damage your eyes if you look at them without protective glasses.

Judaism also began in the ancient Middle East. This religion predates Christianity and shares some teachings with it. For instance, both religions are based on the first section of the Bible, called the Old Testament or Hebrew Bible. The Book of Revelation is not part of Jewish tradition, nor is the story of Armageddon and the Apocalypse. But the Hebrew Bible does mention a Day of the Lord, on which God causes death and destruction to nonbelievers. It also describes the War of Gog and Magog—a battle between good and evil. These events are similar to the Christian Apocalypse. They too end with the death of all nonbelievers and eternal life for believers.

Islam is a religion that developed on the Arabian Peninsula in the A.D. 600s. It is based on the teachings of a man named Muhammad. The Islamic religion views Jesus as an important prophet but not as the son of God. The Islamic end-of-the-world story says that someday Jesus will return to the Middle East to slay an Antichrist, or force of evil. Forty years later, Jesus will die a natural death. After that, the world will end. Everyone will die except Islamic believers, who will receive eternal life.

TALL TALES

Many novelists have written about the end of the world or at least the end of the human race. Some writers envision an epidemic—or widespread disease outbreak—that kills nearly everyone on Earth. In 1826 British author Mary Shelley (most famous for writing *Frankenstein*) published *The Last Man*. This novel tells the story of the only person to survive a worldwide disease outbreak. *The Scarlet Plague* (1912) by U.S. author Jack London tells how a handful of survivors attempt to rebuild civilization, also after a worldwide epidemic. *The Earth Abides* (1949) by U.S. writer George R. Stewart tells a similar story. *The Stand* (1977), by U.S. horror writer Stephen King, is about the aftermath of a global influenza, or flu, epidemic.

In other novels, something—or someone—from space brings about the end of the world or humanity. In his 1893 novel *Omega: The Last Days of the World*, French astronomer (space scientist) Nicolas-Camille Flammarion tells about a comet—an icy body flying through space—that hits Earth. In his 1898 novel *The War of the Worlds*, British author H. G. Wells tells of the near-destruction of humanity by invaders from Mars. In *The Second Deluge*, a 1912 novel by U.S. science writer Garrett Serviss, Earth passes through a giant cloud of water in space. The cloud floods the entire Earth and drowns millions. One of the most famous end-of-the-world books is *When Worlds Collide*. Written in 1933 by Americans Edwin Balmer and Philip Wylie, it tells what happens before and after Earth collides with another planet.

During World War II (1939–1945), the United States developed a new type of deadly weapon—nuclear, or atomic, bombs. Near the end of the war (which pitted the United States and its allies against Germany, Japan, and their allies), the United States

This illustration appeared in H. G. Wells's 1898 novel *The War of the Worlds*. In this scene, a Martian fighting machine attacks human civilization near the Thames River in London, England.

dropped nuclear bombs on two Japanese cities. The bombs destroyed both cities and killed tens of thousands of people. After the war, the Soviet Union (fifteen republics that included Russia) and the United States became bitter enemies. They began to stockpile thousands of nuclear weapons. People worried that a new world war might break out, this time fought with nuclear bombs. Many authors wrote about the possibility. One of the most famous of these books is *A Canticle for Leibowitz* (1959) by U.S. writer Walter M. Miller. It is set in a small monastery, or religious community, in the U.S. Southwest following a worldwide nuclear war. Over hundreds of years,

A mushroom cloud fills the sky after the United States dropped an atomic bomb on the city of Nagasaki, Japan, near the end of World War II in 1945.

the monks who live there try to preserve human knowledge so they can re-create civilization.

In the twenty-first century, novelists have grappled with additional end-of-the-world scenarios. For example, U.S. writer James Howard Kunstler has set a number of novels, including *World Made by Hand* (2009) and *The Witch of Hebron* (2010), in a United States that has used up all its petroleum—the oil that powers cars and many other machines. Because the modern world relies so heavily on petroleum, global businesses and the worldwide economy fall into chaos when the supply runs out. The characters in Kunstler's novels are forced to cope with this dilemma and create a new kind of society.

THE END ON THE BIG SCREEN

The end of the world has been a popular subject for movies. In 1916 Danish filmmakers made a science-fiction movie called *The End of the World* (*Verdens undergang* in Danish). In this story, a comet flies extremely close to Earth, causing vast storms, giant ocean waves, and other destruction.

A 1934 French film was also called *The End of the World* (*La Fin du Monde* in French). This film, too, deals with a comet hurtling toward Earth. *When Worlds Collide* (1953) is based on the 1933 novel of the same name. It tells of a small band of humans who escape Earth in a rocket ship right before a collision with another planet. The film ends with the destruction of the entire Earth.

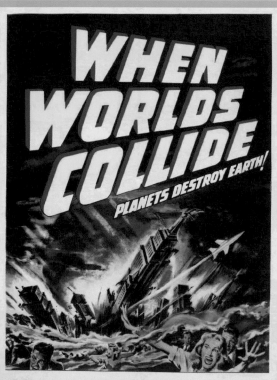

This movie poster advertises *When Worlds Collide* (1953). The film won an Academy Award for its special effects.

After World War II, Hollywood filmmakers made many movies about nuclear war. *On the Beach* (1959), based on a novel by British writer Nevil Shute, tells of Australians who escape the destruction of a nuclear war in the nations to the north. But they can't escape the fallout—or deadly debris—

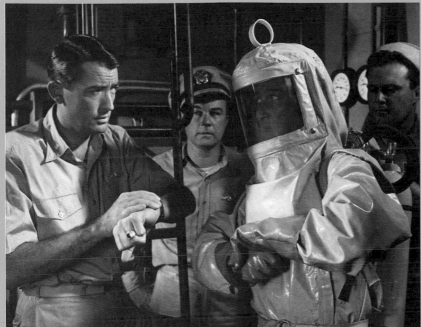

As the United States and the Soviet Union stockpiled nuclear bombs after World War II, Hollywood screenwriters explored the threat of nuclear war. Films such as *On the Beach (top)* and *Fail-Safe (bottom)* warned of nuclear destruction.

that travels through the air after nuclear explosions. *Fail-Safe* (1964) examines the dilemma of U.S. leaders after a U.S. plane is accidentally sent to drop a nuclear bomb on Moscow, Russia, the capital of the Soviet Union. *Dr. Strangelove* (1964), from acclaimed American filmmaker Stanley Kubrick, uses black humor to examine the end of the world.

Above: Dr. Strangelove (1964) is a dark comedy about nuclear war. In this still from the movie, Major T. J. "King" Kong, rides a nuclear bomb on its way to Earth. *Below:* An enormous tsunami (gigantic ocean wave), caused by a comet slamming into Earth, hits the shores of New York City in the 1998 film *Deep Impact.*

The film includes a host of eccentric characters, including a deranged military officer who accidentally starts a nuclear war.

Modern filmmakers continue to explore end-of-the-world scenarios. *The Quiet Earth* (1985) is a New Zealand movie about the only survivors of a strange event that has wiped almost all human life from the planet. *In Deep Impact* (1998), a comet is hurtling through space toward Earth. People must act quickly to destroy the comet before it hits. In *The Core* (2003), Earth is about to lose its magnetic field, an invisible shield that protects us from deadly particles from the Sun. Scientists must travel to Earth's core, or interior, to save living things.

In the film *2012* (2009), violent storms on the Sun have led

to a heating up of Earth's core. The heat has made Earth's crust, or outer layer, unstable—which could mean worldwide destruction. As scientists scramble to save the human race, earthquakes strike and volcanoes erupt all over Earth.

In the 2011 film *Battle: Los Angeles,* thousands of meteors seem to be raining down on Earth, causing worldwide destruction. But it soon becomes clear that the objects are not meteors but missiles from alien invaders. It falls to one platoon of U.S. Marines to save humanity.

CHAPTER 2
2012

Every so often, an end-of-the-world theory grabs a lot of public attention. Most recently, some people have claimed that the world will end on December 21, 2012. The prediction is a complicated combination of ideas that began in the twentieth century.

Beginning in 1976, a U.S. author named Zecharia Sitchin (1920–2010) wrote a series of books. In them, he claimed that the solar system (the Sun and all the planets that travel around it) contains a mysterious extra planet called Nibiru, or Planet X. He based this idea on the myths, writings, and artwork of the ancient Mesopotamians, people who lived in the Middle East about five thousand years ago. Sitchin claimed that Nibiru has an unusual orbit, or path through space, and that it travels through the solar system every thirty-six hundred years. When this happens, according to Sitchin, Nibiru comes very near Earth. As it zooms past, it causes worldwide earthquakes, volcanoes, hurricanes, tornadoes, and tidal waves (gigantic ocean waves).

Sitchin won many followers. One of them, a woman who claimed to communicate with beings from other planets, said that Nibiru was due to hit Earth in May 2003. But May 2003 came and went and nothing unusual happened. So supporters of the Nibiru theory pushed the date back. They said Nibiru was actually going to crash into Earth in December 2012.

Archaeologists have learned much about the ancient Mayan culture by deciphering the pictures they carved into rocks. The Mayans created calendars to keep track of time and special dates. Did the ancient Mayans foretell the end of time?

SCIENTISTS SAY NO

Supporters of the Nibiru theory claim that astronomers, including those at the U.S. National Aeronautics and Space Administration (NASA), have already sighted and photographed Nibiru. But astronomers say that's not true. Every night, tens of thousands of amateur astronomers watch the skies all over the world. Not one of them has reported seeing an extra planet.

Believers in Nibiru say the planet is nearly as big as Jupiter, the largest planet in our solar system. If that's the case, however, and if Nibiru is due to arrive in

A REAL PLANET X

The fact that Nibiru is sometimes called Planet X has caused confusion. Astronomers often use the letter X for objects that are unknown or hypothetical (believed but not yet proved to exist). For instance, astronomers referred to Pluto as Planet X when they were searching for it in the early 1900s. Modern astronomers use the same term for bodies orbiting beyond Pluto. These Planet Xs have nothing to do with Nibiru.

Powerful telescopes, such as this one at the top of Mauna Kea, a volcanic mountain in Hawaii, help scientists look at our solar system and beyond. If a planet larger than Jupiter were lurking in our solar system, astronomers would know it. Some end-of-the-world theorists say a rogue planet could enter Earth's orbit and bring an end to our planet.

Jupiter

Saturn

Mars

Venus

Mercury

People can see the planets Jupiter, Saturn, Mars, Venus, and Mercury from Earth using nothing but binoculars on a clear night. You can't see Nibiru because there is no such planet.

2012, we would surely be able to see the planet by now. After all, at its nearest approach to Earth, Jupiter is clearly visible to the naked eye. And when viewed through even a small telescope or pair of binoculars, Jupiter looks large and clear. If Nibiru is on its way, we'd be able to see it—even in daytime. But in fact, no one has seen Nibiru.

Some supporters of the Nibiru theory say it can't be seen because it is on the other side of the Sun. But Earth and all other planets (including Nibiru, if it exists) orbit the Sun. They are like cars racing around a racetrack. Each car is traveling at a different speed. This means the planets are constantly catching up with and passing one another. Anything that is behind the Sun now will be visible in just a month or so as Earth moves along in its orbit and catches up with it. So Nibiru, if it were behind the Sun, wouldn't stay hidden for very long.

Astronomers say there's no such planet as Nibiru. And they have plenty of science to back them up. For one thing, the gravity, or attraction, of each planet in the solar system affects all the other planets. The closer two planets are to each other, the more they affect each other. For instance, when the planet Neptune approaches the planet Uranus, the pull of Neptune's gravity slows Uranus down slightly. A planet the size of Nibiru— or even one a lot smaller—would affect the paths of other planets as it passed through the solar system. It would be like a car suddenly crossing all the lanes of a busy highway. But there have been no disturbances in the orbits of other planets. They are calmly sailing along through space, exactly as they should be.

THE MAYAN PROPHECY

People who think the world will end in 2012 use another argument as well. They point to the calendar of the ancient Maya. The Mayan people lived in Mexico and Central America from about 1000 B.C. to about A.D. 900. The Maya had a sophisticated society. They built big cities, created fine artwork, used a complex written language, and developed systems of mathematics and astronomy.

Like people in many societies, the Maya also created a calendar. They kept track of periods of time, just as we keep track of years, decades, and centuries. The longest Mayan period—called a *baktun*—lasted about 394 years.

Some Mayan writings suggest that each cycle of thirteen baktuns had special significance in the Mayan religion. In 1975 a U.S. writer named Frank Waters used this idea to come up with his own theory. In his book *Mexico Mystique*, Waters falsely claimed that in Mayan mythology, each thirteen-baktun cycle brought about the destruction and rebirth of the world. Waters said that the current cycle would end on December 24, 2011. On that date, he said, the world would be destroyed by tremendous earthquakes.

In *The Invisible Landscape*, also published in 1975, U.S. brothers Dennis and Terence McKenna described another Mayan end-of-the-world prophecy (prediction), which they also made up. But these writers came up with a slightly different date:

Maya Cosmogenesis 2012, published in 1995, convinced some people that the end of the world was near.

December 21, 2012. The McKennas said the disaster to occur on that date would be caused by a mysterious relationship between Earth and the Milky Way galaxy (a giant group of stars, gas, dust, and other matter, including the Sun and our solar system).

For twenty years, most people ignored these predictions. Then, in 1995, U.S. author John Major Jenkins combined the earlier ideas into a book called *Maya Cosmogenesis 2012*. On December 21 of that year, Jenkins declared, the winter Sun would appear to cross over the center of the Milky Way. He said this event would cause great disasters on Earth, though he didn't explain how.

By this time, many people had jumped on board the 2012 bandwagon. Although historians and scientists pointed out all the falsehoods and errors in the predictions, some people still believed them. Some people pointed to the Mayan calendar itself as proof. They claimed, again falsely, that the Mayan calendar ends with the year 2012, with nothing listed beyond it. They said this indicates that the Maya expected the world to end then.

Once again, scholars pointed out the error in this theory. In fact, experts noted that one Mayan text talks about a celebration scheduled for October 15, 4772. If the Maya were planning that far ahead, it's clear that they didn't think the end of the world would come in 2012.

People prepared for the end of the world in ancient times, and they still do so in the twenty-first century.

COMBINING DISASTERS

Eventually, some believers combined the idea of the Mayan prophecy with catastrophes caused by the planet Nibiru. They suggested that the ancient Mayans somehow knew of this planet and had calculated the date of its approach to Earth.

Believers in the imaginary planet Nibiru think it will make a close approach to Earth. When this happens, they say, catastrophes like the one illustrated here will envelope the planet.

If you search the Internet, you will find millions of websites discussing these theories. To counteract the falsehoods, NASA and other organizations have created informational Web pages of their own. One site, www.2012hoax.org, is subtitled "Debunking the '2012 Doomsday.'" *Doomsday* is another name for a time of great death and destruction. The site warns people: "Don't be scammed."

A massive earthquake struck the South American country of Chile in March 2010. Earthquakes can cause massive destruction—but not on a worldwide scale.

CHAPTER 3
PSEUDOSCIENCE

Many people who prophesy (predict) the end of the world do so on scientific grounds—or at least they think their reasons are scientific. Sciencelike theories that are not supported by accepted scientific methodology are called pseudoscience. *Pseudo* comes from a Greek word that means "to lie." Astrology—a practice based on the belief that the movements and relationships of the planets and stars affect people's lives—is an example of a pseudoscience. Many end-of-the world theories are also based on pseudoscience.

SHIFTING CRUST

One pseudoscientific end-of-the-world theory came from Charles Hapgood, a U.S. history professor. In 1958 he wrote a book called *Earth's Shifting Crust*. In it he said that Earth's crust might slide around, or slip, "much as the skin of an orange, were it loose, might shift over the inner part of the orange all in one piece." Such an event would cause worldwide destruction, Hapgood said. Giant waves would sweep across the oceans, and mountains would come crashing down. Earthquakes would strike, and volcanoes would erupt. But this wouldn't be just localized destruction. According to Hapgood, the disasters would happen everywhere on Earth.

Why would Earth's crust suddenly slip? Hapgood said that if too much ice piled up at the North Pole or the South Pole, the extra weight might throw the crust out of balance. Hapgood predicted the slip for the early decades of the twenty-first century.

5/5/2000: A FAILED PROPHECY

In 1986 an author named Richard Noone published a best-selling book. Titled *5/5/2000*, it predicted that the end of the world would occur on May 5, 2000. Noone said that the ice mass that covers Antarctica would be 3 miles (5 kilometers) thick on May 5, 2000—more than twice its normal thickness. Also on this date, according to Noone, all the planets would be positioned in a straight line. Their gravity, the author claimed, combined with the excess weight of Antarctic ice, would cause the entire globe to flip onto its side, resulting in devastating earthquakes and tsunamis. Rather than look to science to support this idea, Noone looked to ancient legends, myths, and Bible stories. But Noone's prophecy was completely wrong. On May 5, 2000, the planets did not align, the ice of Antarctica was not 3 miles thick, and the globe kept spinning as usual.

Although a few people paid attention to Hapgood and his book, scientists pretty much ignored his ideas. They knew that Hapgood's theory was flawed. Instead of being one giant piece, like the skin of an orange, scientists were learning that Earth's crust is formed of many separate pieces. Called tectonic plates, these pieces can be thought of as giant rafts. Each plate floats on top of the semimolten (partially melted) rock beneath it, like ice floating on a pond. As the plates slowly drift around the surface of Earth, the continents move along with them.

The tectonic plates move about 0.8 to 4 inches (2 to 10 centimeters) a year. Occasionally, when two plates rub against or bump into each other, earthquakes result. Earthquakes can cause great destruction. For instance, an earthquake and the resulting fires destroyed the city of San Francisco, California, in 1906. In 1994 an earthquake in Los Angeles, California, killed thirty-three people, injured nine thousand more, and caused more than $20 billion in damage. But no matter how major, earthquakes are always localized—or confined to a single place.

California sits on a fault line—the meeting place of two tectonic plates. It has been the site of many earthquakes, including a 1906 San Francisco quake *(top)* and a 1994 Los Angeles quake *(bottom)*.

Earth's tectonic plates move independently of one another, not all together. Hapgood's idea of the entire crust shifting at once was based on a faulty understanding of Earth science and was therefore pure fantasy.

PLANETARY ALIGNMENT

Another pseudoscientific end-of-the-world idea is that of planetary alignment. This is the belief that as the planets travel around the Sun, they occasionally line up. Imagine cars racing in circles around a central point, each car farther away from the middle than the next. Some cars are moving fast, and others are moving slowly. Since all the cars are moving at different speeds, it makes sense to think that sometimes—just for a moment—they will all line up in a straight line, from the center on out.

All objects, including the Sun, the Moon, and the planets, have gravity. The Sun's gravity pulls on the planets, keeping them in orbit. The Moon's gravity pulls on Earth, Earth's gravity

An illustration depicts some of the planets in our solar system orbiting the Sun. The picture shows the planets in nearly a straight line, which some people believe would lead to disaster on Earth. However, it would be impossible for all the planets to line up this way.

One writer predicted that the planets would all line up on May 5, 2000. This illustration shows the actual position of the planets on that day.

pulls on the Moon, and all the other planets and moons pull on one another. The planets are much smaller than the Sun, so their gravitational pull on the Sun is weak. But people have wondered: What if all the planets lined up in a straight line projecting out from the Sun? Would their *combined* gravitational pull have an effect on the Sun? Imagine a heavy weight with nine ropes attached. If nine people pulled on those ropes in nine different directions, the weight would go nowhere. But if there were just one rope and all nine people pulled on it at the same time and in the same direction, the weight would move easily.

In 1974 two British physicists and astronomers, John Gribbin and Stephen Plagemann, wrote a book based on this idea. Called *The Jupiter Effect*, it argued that the combined gravity of all the planets pulling in the same line would affect the Sun. The authors thought the Sun would respond to this increased pull with increased surface activity, such as sunspots and solar flares. Increased surface activity on the Sun causes an increase in the solar wind, a stream of particles that flow into space from the Sun.

Promoters of the planetary alignment theory predicted tsunamis (as occurred in Japan after a massive earthquake in March 2011; *top*) and volcanoes *(as shown above)* for March 10, 1982. But the planets didn't line up and nothing dramatic happened on that day.

The solar wind can affect weather on Earth. For example, an increase in the solar wind can cause Earth's atmosphere, the layer of gases around Earth, to warm up. The extra warmth can cause strong hurricanes and other storms.

Gribbin and Plagemann believed that an increase in the solar wind caused by planetary alignment would have an even greater effect. They thought the increase would alter the rate at which Earth rotates, or spins around. They thought variations in Earth's rotation would cause massive earthquakes, volcanoes, and tsunamis.

MORE BIG QUAKES?

Some people say that the number of big earthquakes has been increasing. They point to massive quakes, such as the one in Japan in March 2011, as an indication that something is going wrong and that the end of the world is near.

But is the number of earthquakes really increasing? Are there more big earthquakes than in the past? The answer is no.

According to the U.S. Geological Survey, a government agency that monitors Earth and the environment, the number of big quakes has remained fairly constant over the past one hundred years. Big quakes may even have decreased in number in recent years.

Still, it may seem as if the number of earthquakes is increasing—for several reasons. One is that scientists are getting much better at detecting earthquakes. They have high-tech equipment, capable of feeling even very small earthquakes. In addition, more and more scientists are looking for earthquakes. More than four thousand earthquake-detecting stations operate around the world. So it is not that more earthquakes are occurring. Scientists are just getting better at noticing them.

In addition, as populations expand, more people are building cities and homes in earthquake-prone areas. So when a major earthquake does occur, it is more likely to cause damage, death, and injuries than earthquakes that occurred twenty or even ten years ago. Buildings in many earthquake zones are not strong enough to withstand quakes. For instance, in 2010 a major earthquake struck the country of Haiti, a poor nation on an island in the Caribbean Sea. The earthquake almost completely destroyed the Haitian capital city of Port-au-Prince. A few months later, an even stronger earthquake struck Chile in South America. Even though this earthquake was much more powerful than the one in Haiti, it caused far less damage. Because Chile is a wealthier nation than Haiti, the people there were able to make many of their buildings earthquake-resistant, which people in Haiti could not afford to do. The earthquake-resistant buildings in Chile weathered the quake, resulting in much less destruction.

The authors predicted that the planets would line up on March 10, 1982. But nothing out of the ordinary happened to Earth that day. Gribbin and Plagemann then tried to explain away the continued existence of the world after March 10. They said the planets actually *had* aligned that day and had an effect on Earth. The effect was just very hard to measure, they said. They went on to suggest that the eruption of Mount Saint Helens, a volcano in Washington State, two years earlier had been triggered by the alignment.

What was wrong with the planetary alignment theory? First and most important, the planets didn't line up on March 10, 1982. On that date, the planets were spread out over about one-quarter of a circle. In fact, most scientists agree that the planets can never completely line up. As each planet orbits the Sun, its gravity tugs, pulls, and nudges other planets. A planet catching up with a slower one will pull on it, slowing it down. A planet passing another will pull on it, speeding it up. All these effects combine to prevent the planets from ever lining up in a straight row.

Even if the planets did line up, there is no evidence they would have any unusual effect on the Sun. The Sun is one thousand times more massive than all the planets combined. Even if they all pulled from the same direction, their gravity would be much too weak to affect the Sun. Furthermore, an increase in the solar wind would have no effect on Earth's rotation. The solar wind is much too weak and thin to affect something as big and massive as our planet. In 1999, years after proposing the planetary alignment theory, John Gribbin himself denounced it. He said, "I don't like it, and I'm sorry I ever had anything to do with it."

POLE SHIFTS

Some doomsayers have predicted that a pole shift—the switching of Earth's north pole and south pole—will bring about the end of the world. A pole shift wouldn't mean the world would turn upside down, although some people have warned of that too. Instead, it means that Earth's *magnetic* poles would change places.

Earth has two types of poles: physical and magnetic. The physical poles are in the Arctic Ocean (the North Pole) and in Antarctica (the South Pole). Like a wheel spinning around on an axle, Earth spins on its axis, an imaginary line running north and south through the planet. At the top of this line is the North Pole. At the bottom is the South Pole.

The magnetic poles are near the physical poles. But they are not fixed in one spot. The magnetic poles mark the bottom and top of Earth's magnetic field. This field is a set of invisible lines around Earth where magnetism can be felt. Magnetism is a force that pulls objects together or pushes them away from one another. If you've ever used a magnet to attach pictures to your refrigerator, you've seen magnetism at work. If you've ever used a pocket compass, you've also seen magnetism at work. The needle on a compass always points toward the magnetic North Pole. Travelers use compasses to figure out whether they're heading north, south, east, or west.

Earth's magnetic field is very important to life. The magnetic field helps shield Earth from the solar wind. Some particles in the solar wind contain deadly radiation. If

If the magnetic north and south poles were to switch (and they have in the past), your compass might not work. But the world would not end.

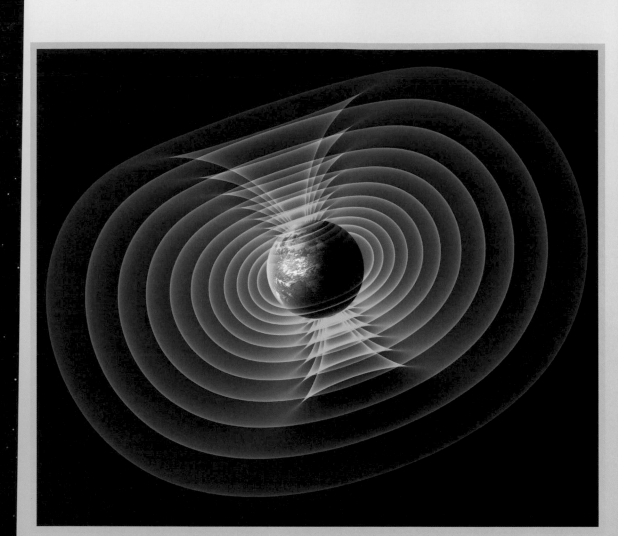

Earth's magnetic field protects us from deadly radiation from the Sun. Even when the field flips, as it has in the past, it does not stop protecting us.

these particles reached the ground, they would kill plants and animals, but Earth's magnetic field causes most of them to swerve harmlessly around the planet.

Proponents of the pole shift theory say that if Earth's north and south magnetic poles ever switched places, the magnetic field would suddenly "turn off," or stop working. This would allow deadly radiation from the Sun to pour onto Earth's surface. The particles would kill most life, including human beings.

In fact, Earth's magnetic field *has* flipped many times in the past. No one knows why the switch happens. But when it does, the north and south magnetic poles trade places. The switch occurs about every two hundred thousand years. The last time

Earth's magnetic field flipped was 780,000 years ago. For this reason, many scientists think Earth is overdue for a flip.

The magnetic field has reversed many thousands of times, including times when plants, human beings, and other animals lived on Earth. The magnetic field did not turn off during these times, and life continued. And even if the magnetic field did turn off, we'd still survive. That's because the magnetic field is not the only shield we have against radiation. Earth's atmosphere is also a very powerful defense. It's as effective at stopping radiation as a wall of concrete 13 feet (4.5 meters) thick.

Large solar flares, also known as solar prominences, throw huge amounts of heat and radiation out into space. An extremely large solar flare could damage and destroy electrical systems on Earth.

CHAPTER 4

KNOCKOUT FROM SPACE

Various end-of-the-world scenarios are based on a faulty understanding of Earth science and astronomy. However, some natural events could destroy Earth—or at least destroy human society as we know it.

POWER PUNCH

The Sun itself could cause the destruction. The Sun sends a tremendous amount of radiation, or energy, to Earth. A lot of this energy is beneficial. For instance, the Sun's energy keeps us warm and allows plants to grow. People and animals rely on plants for food.

On the other hand, the Sun also sends a lot of dangerous radiation toward Earth. Most of this radiation never reaches Earth's surface. Two barriers protect us from the Sun's dangerous radiation. The first is Earth's atmosphere, which filters out some of the most dangerous radiation from the Sun. This radiation includes ultraviolet (UV) light, which can cause skin cancer and other health problems. The second barrier is Earth's magnetic field. It protects us from other types of dangerous radiation.

Sometimes solar flares (extra-powerful eruptions of gases on the Sun) send greater than normal amounts of radiation to Earth. Although the atmosphere protects living things from this radiation, it can still penetrate Earth's magnetic shield. And because the particles in the radiation are electrical, they can damage electrical and electronic devices in space. For instance, the energy from solar flares can damage electronic components in satellites, or spacecraft that orbit Earth's atmosphere. Astronauts in space, above the protection of Earth's atmosphere, might also receive harmful amounts of radiation during solar flares. For this reason, the International Space Station (ISS), which serves as an outer space home to astronauts from around the world for long periods, has a special extra-protective room. It shields astronauts from radiation during solar flares.

Sometimes energy from a solar flare damages electronic devices on Earth. For instance, in 1972 a giant solar flare knocked out long-distance telephone communication across the U.S. state of Illinois. A solar flare in 1989 shut down electrical power in the Canadian province of Quebec. The incident left six million people in darkness for nine hours. In 2005 another solar flare disrupted the worldwide Global Positioning System (GPS) for ten minutes. Businesses and organizations around

Crew members aboard the International Space Station gather in one of the station's laboratories. Because the ISS is above Earth's atmosphere, its astronauts need special protection during solar flares.

SPACE WEATHER WATCHERS

There is no way to prevent a solar flare, but we can prevent most of the damage that solar flares can cause on Earth. The National Oceanographic and Atmospheric Administration (NOAA) is the U.S. government agency in charge of keeping track of the weather. It also keeps track of "space weather," such as solar wind and solar flares. NOAA's Space Weather Prediction Center monitors the Sun and watches for solar flares. It gathers information using satellites and a worldwide network of ground-based observatories. When solar flares occur, the agency sends out warnings to businesses and governments. Operators place satellites on standby so that electrically charged particles from the Sun do not damage their delicate electronics. Electric companies activate special devices to protect power lines and other equipment. Airlines and shipping companies also take steps to protect their navigation and computer equipment.

Radar/Warning Forecaster

U.S. government scientists don't just study weather on Earth. They also study dangerous "space weather," such as solar flares.

the world—everything from trucking companies to airlines to armies—depend on GPS for navigation, or finding locations on Earth. A longer breakdown of the GPS might be disastrous. It could bring business and government to a standstill.

SUPERFLARE

On the morning of September 1, 1859, thirty-three-year-old British astronomer Richard Carrington was observing the Sun with a telescope. He noticed a large group of dark patches on the

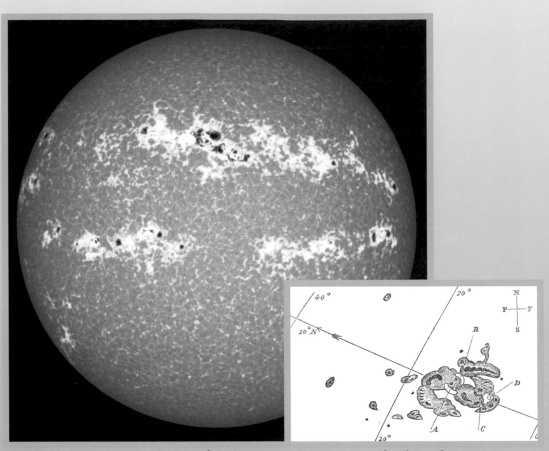

Top: The dark spots on the Sun's surface, known as sunspots, are cooler than other areas on the Sun. *Inset:* Astronomer Richard Carrington made this picture of bright sunspots in 1859. The spots were accompanied that year by a huge solar flare.

Sun's surface. The patches were sunspots, or magnetic whirlpools on the Sun. Sunspots are accompanied by solar flares and other violent storms on the Sun. While Carrington was watching, two blinding spots of white light suddenly appeared over the sunspots. These spots quickly grew brighter. Carrington had seen a gigantic solar flare. By the time he could call for someone to witness what he'd seen, the sunspots and the solar flare were almost gone.

Just before dawn the next day, skies all over Earth were filled with red, green, and purple auroras—or lights in the sky. The auroras resulted from massive numbers of electrical particles from the solar flare hitting Earth's magnetic field. The lights were so bright that people could read newspapers by them. Normally auroras appear only at the North Pole and the South

Pole. But on this day, auroras filled the skies everywhere.

At the same time, telegraph systems, a form of electrical communication used in the nineteenth and early twentieth century, went haywire worldwide. Powerful sparks shot from telegraphic instruments, electrically shocking the people who operated them. Even after telegraph operators disconnected their machines, electric current still flowed through the systems. The Carrington Flare, as the eruption came to be called, was the largest, most powerful solar flare ever observed.

In 1859 people were just learning about the uses of electricity. Other than telegraph systems, few other electrical devices could be damaged by the Carrington Flare. But what would happen if a similar flare occurred in the twenty-first century, when people around the world rely so much on electrical devices in their everyday lives? If a similar flare occurred, power lines would explode and electrical generating

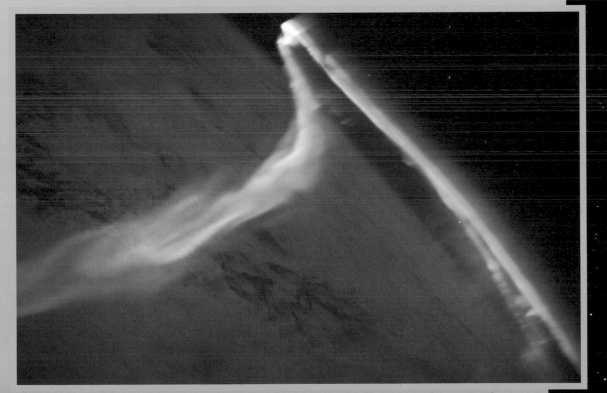

When electrical particles generated during a solar flare hit Earth's magnetic field, they put on an impressive light show known as an aurora. In May 2010, astronauts aboard the ISS photographed this aurora from space.

plants would shut down. In your home and in offices and businesses, electrical circuits would blow out and wiring would burn up. Every electronic device—cash registers, refrigerators, and lighting systems—would stop working. Computers would be useless boxes full of electronic gadgets and wires. The damage would affect most places on Earth and go beyond Earth. The flare would damage or destroy electrical equipment in space satellites. Everything from satellite communication systems to GPS would fail.

Suppose it took weeks or even months to repair the damage. Without electric lights, our homes would be dark at night. Stoves wouldn't work, making it hard to cook food. Refrigerators and freezers wouldn't work, so we couldn't store foods safely. Electric heaters wouldn't work, so many people would be cold. Hospitals would go dark. All the machines hospitals use to operate on and care for patients would be useless. Without these machines, some patients would die.

Battery-operated flashlights, radios, power generators, and other devices would run for a little while, but people would have no way to recharge the batteries once they ran out of power. Would it be the end of the world? No. But it would be the end of life as we know it for quite a long time.

EARTH GRAZERS

Solar flares are not the only danger from space. Asteroids also pose a threat to Earth and everything that lives here. Asteroids are rocky objects that travel through space. They can be as big as a house or a small mountain. Sometimes asteroids skim over Earth's atmosphere, skipping off it like a stone skipping across water in a pond. But if an asteroid is big enough, it can punch right through the atmosphere and reach Earth's surface. For instance, about fifty thousand years ago, a large asteroid hit the desert in modern-day Arizona. The asteroid was about 150 feet (50 m) wide. The impact created a hole 4,000 feet

(1,200 m) across and 570 feet (170 m) deep. This is deeper than the Washington Monument is tall. (The crater hasn't changed much in the last fifty thousand years. Modern scientists go to the Arizona desert to study the crater. It's also a popular tourist attraction.)

About fifty thousand years ago, an asteroid crashed in the Arizona desert, creating a huge crater *(above)*. The illustration below shows asteroids streaking toward Earth. But in reality, the chances of a major asteroid strike are very small.

BOMBS BURSTING IN AIR

On June 30, 1908, a ball of fire suddenly lit up the sky over a remote region of Siberia, in northeastern Russia. Witnesses as far as 240 miles (386 km) away reported a flash as bright as the Sun. "The whole northern part of the sky," said one witness, "appeared covered with fire. . . . At that moment there was a bang in the sky, and a mighty crash. . . . I was thrown twenty feet (6 m) from the porch. . . . The earth trembled." Seismometers—instruments used for detecting earthquakes— as far away as 600 miles (965 km) recorded the explosion. People 300 miles (500 km) away heard the sound and saw the sky light up. The explosion completely flattened part of a forest (below) and set the rest on fire. It knocked down houses and killed hundreds of reindeer.

What happened that day? Because of the remoteness of the region and the political turmoil in Russia during that era, it was decades before an expedition reached the site. Investigators were astonished by what they found. Tens of thousands of trees lay flat on the ground. They all pointed away from a central spot. It looked as though a huge explosion had knocked them down. Scientists thought an asteroid had hit the spot. But there was no crater—the normal result of such a collision. How could an object hit Earth and cause such devastation yet leave no crater?

Scientists figured out that the object never reached the ground. It exploded high in the air over Siberia. Modern scientists believe the object was a small asteroid or large meteoroid (similar to an asteroid but smaller). It was probably only about 10 to 20 feet (3 to 6 m) wide, about the size of a small house. But it exploded with the force of a nuclear bomb. Siberia is a remote region, without a lot of people, so no people were killed.

Similar explosions have occurred in recent times. For instance, on October 8, 2009, an asteroid about 30 feet (10 m) across exploded over Indonesia, a nation in Southeast Asia. The explosion was about twice as powerful as one of the nuclear bombs dropped in World War II. Just over a month later, another small asteroid exploded over Utah in the western United States. The explosion occurred at midnight. For a brief moment, the landscape was lit as bright as day. Because these events occurred high in Earth's atmosphere, they did no damage to things on the ground.

Thousands of asteroids travel through the solar system all the time. Most orbit the Sun between the orbits of Mars and Jupiter. This region of space is called the asteroid belt. But not all asteroids are in this belt. Some travel elsewhere in the solar system.

In 1932 scientists discovered an asteroid that crosses Earth's orbit about every two years. They named it 1862 Apollo. After that, all asteroids that cross Earth's orbit have been called Apollo asteroids. Scientists have found more than 260 Apollo asteroids. The biggest is 1036 Ganymed. It is nearly 19 miles (30 km) across. The next largest is 1862 Apollo itself, at 6 miles (10 km) wide by 19 miles long.

Some Apollo asteroids pass very close to Earth—so close that we call them Earth grazers. In September 2010, two small asteroids passed less than 120,000 miles (193,000 km) from Earth. That's about half the distance between Earth and the Moon. But some Earth grazers have come even closer. Some have hit Earth.

Asteroids can cross Earth's path in one of two ways. First, they can fly above or below Earth's orbit. This is like a car crossing a railroad track by passing over it on a bridge or under it through a tunnel. Both Apollo and Ganymed travel this way. But other asteroids cross Earth right at the level of its orbit, like a car crossing railroad tracks at ground level. The only asteroids that can hit Earth are those that cross its path this way.

WIPEOUT

About 65.5 million years ago, an asteroid 6 miles (10 km) wide hit the coast of the Yucatán Peninsula in modern-day Mexico. It blasted a crater 190 miles (300 km) wide and 9 to 16 miles (15 to 25 km) deep. The impact created earthquakes of extreme violence. A tsunami up to 3 miles (5 km) high swept over nearby low-lying land.

Within an hour of the impact, millions of tons of red-hot debris from the explosion began to fall back to Earth. This rain of fire ignited forests worldwide. Fires raged for months, destroying plants and animals and pouring vast clouds of smoke into the sky.

In this artwork *(above)*, an enormous asteroid slams into Earth. Such a collision may have caused the mass extinction of the dinosaurs *(below)* 65 million years ago.

The explosion also converted much of the gases nitrogen and oxygen in Earth's atmosphere into nitrogen oxides. These chemicals mixed with water vapor inside clouds. When rain fell, it was deadly acid rain, which killed more plant and animal life.

Meanwhile, vast amounts of dust and smoke billowed into the upper atmosphere. A layer of dust blanketed Earth. It blocked out the Sun's light and heat. Earth grew dark and cold. Without sunlight, plants died. And without plants to eat, animals died. The dead included the biggest, most successful animals that had ever lived on Earth up to that time: dinosaurs. Another 65 to 70 percent of all life on Earth died out as well.

Although a few scientists question this scenario, Earth holds a lot of evidence to support it. For instance, scientists have discovered the crater itself, buried deep beneath the surface of the sea off the coast of Yucatán. And when the explosion occurred,

SUPERVOLCANOES

Asteroid strikes are not the only things that can throw great amounts of debris into the air, blocking out the Sun's light. Supervolcanoes can do the same thing. Volcanoes are places where magma (melted rock) from deep inside Earth rises to the surface. When magma reaches the surface, we call it lava. Sometimes lava simply flows slowly from a volcano. Other times, the volcano erupts violently, sending lava, gas, smoke, dust, and rock into the air.

The largest volcanoes are called supervolcanoes. They are thousands of times larger than ordinary volcanoes, and they can send thousands of times more material into the air when they erupt. Earth has six known supervolcanoes. One is beneath Yellowstone National Park in the western United States. The last supervolcano eruption occurred nearly thirty thousand years ago in New Zealand. No one knows when the next will occur. It could be tomorrow, or it could be in ten thousand years. But if a supervolcano does erupt, the debris from the eruption would probably block out sunlight and lead to the death of plants and animals on Earth.

A COSMIC SHOOTING GALLERY

Asteroids and comets sometimes hit other planets in our solar system. One of the most famous was Comet Shoemaker-Levy 9, which traveled toward Jupiter in 1993. As the comet approached, Jupiter's powerful gravity broke it up into numerous small pieces. These pieces eventually collided with the planet in a series of powerful explosions. The impacts left enormous black blotches on the cloud tops of Jupiter. Each of these blotches was larger than the entire planet Earth.

In July 2009, an asteroid about 1,600 feet (488 m) wide crashed into Jupiter *(illustration below)*. The impact resulted in a bright flash, which was caught on film by an amateur astronomer in Australia. The impact left a mark the size of the Pacific Ocean on Jupiter.

it blew large amounts of the element iridium into the air. This element is rare on Earth but is common in meteoroids and asteroids. The iridium fell to the ground, creating a thin layer of iridium-rich clay in many places on Earth. This iridium layer dates to around 65.5 million years ago—providing more evidence for the asteroid strike.

COULD IT HAPPEN AGAIN?

The largest of Earth grazers is called Ivar. It is about 5 miles (8 km) wide—almost as big as the asteroid that hit the Yucatán. If Ivar or another big asteroid were to strike Earth, the result would be a global disaster such as the one that wiped out the dinosaurs.

Most Earth grazers are not as large as Ivar. Most are less than 1.25 miles (2 km) wide. But even if one of these were to hit Earth, it could still wipe out an entire city or town. If it hit a populated area such as New York City, the deaths and damage would be staggering.

Scientists know that one day an Earth grazer will hit our planet. But no one knows when. The strike might come tomorrow. It might come in one hundred thousand years, or it might come in sixty-five million years. Asteroids don't travel on schedules, like trains or buses, and there's no way to predict a collision.

AVERTING DISASTER

Asteroids that come near or strike Earth don't arrive with much warning. For instance, scientists detected the two small asteroids that passed near Earth in 2010 only four days ahead

Even a small meteor impact could be devastating. This illustration shows what might happen if a meteor the size of the one that created Meteor Crater in Arizona were to strike New York City.

of time. People at NASA and foreign space agencies are working to develop better warning systems so they can detect asteroids earlier.

But what good does it do to know an asteroid is headed toward Earth? Just knowing about a collision ahead of time doesn't prevent it from happening. So scientists are trying to figure out how to destroy or divert asteroids before they strike. We might be able to destroy an oncoming asteroid by shooting at it with rockets armed with powerful explosives. The explosion that resulted would need to be strong enough to break the asteroid into tiny pieces. If the asteroid broke into larger pieces, the problem might get worse. Several pieces might still hit Earth, giving us many impacts to worry about instead of just one.

Another way to avoid an impact would be to make the asteroid miss Earth entirely. If we intercepted an asteroid

If an asteroid were heading toward us, we might be able to divert it with explosives or rockets, as shown in this illustration.

early enough, it would take only a slight nudge to steer it away from Earth. We might be able to nudge it by setting off small explosions on one side of it or by mounting a rocket engine on its side. This solution also has problems. For one thing, we would need to detect the asteroid very early—when it was still millions of miles from Earth—so that we would have enough time to act. But detecting asteroids that far away is difficult, since most asteroids are not very large, and the farther away they are, the harder they are to see. So far, scientists have sent only a few space missions to asteroids. All of them took years of planning and many months of traveling through space. If an asteroid is discovered to be on a collision course with Earth, we might not have enough time to stop it.

KILLER RAYS

When some large stars die, they do so in a gigantic explosion called a supernova. Supernovas are so powerful that for a short time, the exploding star can outshine an entire galaxy containing billions of stars. Under certain conditions, all that energy can be concentrated into a tight beam, like a searchlight. This beam of energy is known as a gamma-ray burst. It can last up to ten seconds. In that short time, the burst releases more energy than the Sun will emit in its entire ten-billion-year lifetime.

What would happen to Earth if one of these gamma-ray bursts were to hit it? Gamma rays are killers. Even a supernova as far as 6,000 light-years from Earth (a light-year is the distance light travels in one year: about 2 trillion miles (3 trillion km)) could wipe out all life on Earth.

We would have very little warning. Astronomers might detect the burst only a few days before it hit. When the energy hit Earth's atmosphere, it would interact with atmospheric gases, creating a tremendously bright flash of light. Anyone looking at the sky during that time would probably be blinded. But most of the energy from the flash would be invisible ultraviolet light.

The intense radiation from a gamma-ray burst, as shown in this illustration, would cause widespread death on Earth.

GAMMA-RAY BURST: HAS IT HAPPENED BEFORE?

About 440 million years ago, a mass extinction—or dying out of life—occurred on Earth. At that time, no animals were living on land. Almost all Earth's life was in the seas. These life-forms were simple organisms, resembling modern coral, oysters, and sea urchins. More than 60 percent of these life-forms died. Some scientists believe this mass extinction was caused by a nearby gamma-ray burst.

Ultraviolet light from the Sun can cause skin cancer. But ultraviolet light from a gamma-ray burst would damage or kill almost all life it touched. The burst would even penetrate hundreds of feet into the oceans, killing deep-sea life.

A gamma-ray burst would quickly kill half of all life on Earth— those living things on the side of the planet facing the burst. With enough advanced warning, people with the money to do so could move to the other side of Earth ahead of time. That way, Earth's bulk would shield them from the dangerous radiation. But a gamma-ray burst would also damage Earth's ozone layer, which helps shield us from the Sun's UV rays. This damage would allow more UV rays to reach Earth and kill more living things. So even people on the side of Earth facing away from the gamma-ray burst would be exposed to deadly UV rays.

Gamma-ray bursts are very rare. They occur in the Milky Way, our galaxy, only once every few million years. A gamma-ray burst capable of hitting Earth probably occurs even less frequently, only once every several hundred million years. So we probably don't have to worry about this end-of-the-world scenario happening in our lifetime.

People have damaged Earth by polluting air, water, and soil. Will human activity one day destroy all life on Earth?

CHAPTER 5

OUR OWN WORST ENEMY

Not every potential global disaster is a natural disaster. In fact, humans may face more danger from themselves than anything nature could do. Certain events could wipe out the human species altogether. More likely, events triggered by human actions might greatly change and diminish the quality of human life.

POLLUTING THE ENVIRONMENT

Every day, humans pollute, or contaminate, the environment. For instance, mines and factories sometimes dump dangerous chemicals into waterways. Farmers use chemical fertilizers to help their plants grow and chemical pesticides to kill insects. But these chemicals can run off farmland into rivers and lakes. Other water pollution comes from oil spills, when petroleum accidentally leaks into the ocean. A 2010 spill, caused by an oil rig explosion, lasted three months and dumped 185 million gallons (700 million liters) of oil into the Gulf of Mexico. Polluted water is not safe for drinking. Water pollution can sicken and kill plants and animals that live in the water.

Air pollution also damages the environment, threatening the health of people and wildlife. Air pollution comes from car exhaust, factories, mines, and other human businesses. The pollution takes the form of gases, as well as tiny particles in the air. Polluted air can cause asthma and other respiratory illnesses in people. It can also sicken and kill plants and animals. One kind of air pollution, acid rain, has killed whole forests.

Pollution might not bring about the end of the world, but it can make our world very unpleasant—and dangerous—to live in. If pollution continues, Earth might no longer be a fit home for living things.

A HOLE IN THE SKY

In the late 1970s, scientists started noticing changes in Earth's ozone layer, which protects us from UV rays from the Sun. They noticed that from August to October each year, the ozone layer over Antarctica became thinner. August through October is the coldest time of year in Antarctica, which is in the Southern Hemisphere (southern half of Earth). Scientists saw that the layer grew thicker again when Antarctica began to warm up in November.

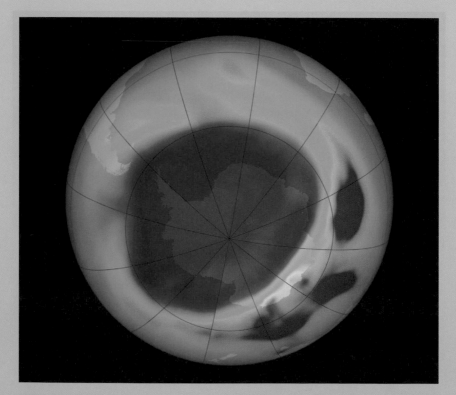

This computer image shows a purple circle indicating lower levels of ozone in Earth's atmosphere over Antarctica. People have taken action to keep the "ozone hole" from getting bigger, but the ozone layer still thins over Antarctica every year.

Scientists traced the thinning ozone layer to air pollution. Human-made chemicals called chlorofluorocarbons (CFCs), combined with cold air in Antarctica, were eating away at the ozone. At the time, CFCs were widely used in air conditioners, refrigerators, aerosol spray cans, foams, and insulating materials.

If the ozone layer were to disappear, we would have no protection from UV rays. Many people would develop skin cancer and cataracts, a clouding of the lenses in the eyes. UV rays can also damage the immune system, which protects people from disease. The rays can also kill animals and plants.

After scientists discovered the "ozone hole," people knew they had to act to protect the ozone layer. In the 1990s, the United States banned CFCs, as did many other countries. Even though CFCs are no longer produced, the ozone layer still thins over Antarctica each year, because old CFC particles remain in the atmosphere.

HOTHOUSE EARTH

Global warming (the increase of Earth's average temperature) is not a future scenario. It is happening and has already started to damage Earth.

Gases in Earth's atmosphere, especially carbon dioxide, act like the glass roof of a greenhouse. This glass allows sunlight in to heat the plants inside but doesn't allow the heat to escape back outside. In the same way, Earth's atmospheric gases allow heat to pass through the atmosphere. The gases also trap some heat near Earth, preventing it from traveling back into space and thereby keeping Earth warm.

In the last one hundred years, the amount of carbon dioxide in Earth's atmosphere has increased. With more carbon dioxide, the atmosphere has been trapping more heat. Where is the extra carbon dioxide coming from? Most of it comes from human activities. Burning fossil fuel releases carbon dioxide into the atmosphere.

GREENHOUSE EFFECT EXPERIMENT

Do the following experiment to learn about the greenhouse effect up close:

SUPPLIES
large glass jar (at least 1 quart, or 1 liter) with a lid
dirt
two household thermometers

STEPS
1. Turn the jar on its side.
2. Scoop in enough dirt to fill about two-thirds of the jar.
3. Lay a thermometer on its side on the dirt and put the lid on the jar.
4. Place the jar, still on its side, outside in direct sunlight.
5. Place the other thermometer alongside the jar.
6. Wait for about an hour.
7. Compare the temperatures.

Your experiment should show that the thermometer inside the jar registers a much higher temperature than the one outside. That's because heat energy from the Sun can pass easily through the glass and into the jar, where it then warms up the dirt. But the heat energy from the dirt is not as strong as the heat energy from the Sun, so it cannot pass back through the glass. It stays trapped inside the jar. Since more heat is coming in than is leaving the jar, the inside of the jar grows hotter than the outside air.

The same thing happens when heat energy passes through the atmosphere and warms Earth. Instead of traveling back out into space, the heat stays trapped near Earth, keeping the planet warm. The more greenhouse gases the atmosphere has, the greater the greenhouse effect.

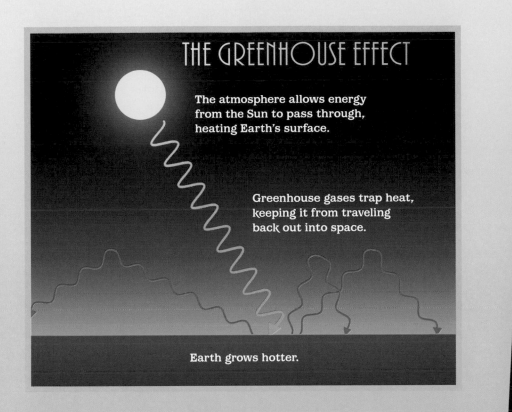

THE GREENHOUSE EFFECT

The atmosphere allows energy from the Sun to pass through, heating Earth's surface.

Greenhouse gases trap heat, keeping it from traveling back out into space.

Earth grows hotter.

People around the world burn a lot of fossil fuels—oil, gas, and coal—to power their cars, warm their houses, operate factories, and power other machines.

A DROWNED PLANET

Because people have burned so much fossil fuel over the years, carbon dioxide levels have increased and Earth has begun to warm. Earth's average temperature has risen 1.33°F (0.74°C) over the past one hundred years. As Earth has warmed, the planet's large ice sheets have begun to melt. These ice sheets cover the Arctic Ocean at the North Pole and the continent of Antarctica at the South Pole. Glaciers, slow-moving ice masses on mountains and in other cold places on Earth, have begun to melt as well.

The melting ice has poured into the world's oceans, causing sea levels to rise. During the twentieth century, sea levels rose between 6 and 8 inches (15 and 20 cm). Many low-lying areas that were once dry land are underwater for most of the year.

FOSSIL FUELS

When people talk about fighting global warming, they often talk about reducing the use of fossil fuels. Fossil fuels are the remains of plants and animals that lived on Earth millions of years ago. Eventually, over the centuries, these remains become buried under layers and layers of soil. Deep beneath the surface of Earth, temperature and pressure (the weight of the soil and rocks above) slowly change the remains into oil, coal, and natural gas. Because they used to be plants and animals, fossil fuels are rich in carbon. When they burn, they combine with oxygen to create carbon dioxide.

These areas include small island nations such as Tuvalu in the Pacific Ocean and the Maldives in the Indian Ocean. In Samoa, also in the Pacific Ocean, many people have had to move their homes farther inland, because the places where they once lived are underwater.

If the melting continues, in a few decades, such island nations as Tuvalu and the Maldives may disappear underwater entirely. Large coastal cities such as New York, New York, and Miami, Florida, might also end up underwater. The floodwaters would drown streets, houses, and buildings. Scientists think that by the end of the twenty-first century, sea levels will have risen another 7 to 23 inches (18 to 59 cm). As a result, up to one billion people might lose their homes to flooding. But it could get even worse. If all the polar ice were to melt, sea levels could rise about 36 feet (12 m).

Rising sea levels can do other kinds of damage as well. Seawater is salty, so it is not fit for humans to drink. As ocean levels rise, seawater could seep into aquifers, or underground pockets of freshwater, from which humans get much of their drinking water. The incoming seawater would make this water unsafe to drink. This situation has already happened on Tuvalu, where freshwater is scarce. People there have to treat seawater to make it drinkable and must ship in freshwater from other places. Scientists warn that by the end of the

The islands and coral reefs that make up Tuvalu in the South Pacific Ocean don't sit high above the water. As sea levels rise due to global warming, this island nation could disappear beneath the ocean.

twenty-first century, three billion people may no longer have access to clean drinking water because of rising sea levels.

MORE REPERCUSSIONS

Global warming has already started to damage wildlife. Ice is composed of freshwater. As polar ice melts, the surrounding seas become warmer and less salty. Many kinds of ocean fish cannot live in the warmer, less salty seas. They have started to die out. Animals such as penguins and polar bears eat fish. But with fewer fish in the sea, they have less food to eat. Without enough food, one species of penguin has already started to die out. Polar bears and penguins also hunt from the thick ice that floats above the polar seas. Without this ice, the animals don't have sufficient hunting grounds. For these reasons, some scientists predict that polar bears and other Arctic animals will soon become extinct.

Global warming is also changing Earth's weather. The Sun's heat provides the energy for wind, blizzards, hurricanes, and other storms. As Earth gets warmer, storms are becoming stronger and more frequent, leading to flooding in some places. The extra warmth is causing water in rivers, lakes, and oceans to evaporate (change into water vapor) more quickly. The extra water vapor in the atmosphere will lead to increased rain and snowfall in some places. Meanwhile, the extra heat and evaporation may leave some places without enough water.

Top: In the Arctic, the normally icy habitat of polar bears has begun to melt. *Bottom:* This illustration shows ocean waters swamping the city of Miami, Florida. If sea levels continue to rise, this scenario could become a reality.

WHAT TO DO?

Some people say that global warming is unstoppable. They say that humans will never stop driving cars, using electricity, and doing other things that emit greenhouse gases. But while humans might not be able to stop global warming, they might be able to keep it from getting worse. For instance, we could slow global warming by using energy more efficiently. We could create more fuel-efficient cars and cars that produce fewer greenhouse gases. We could increase our use of wind and solar power, which don't produce greenhouse gases.

Plants can play a role in slowing global warming. Plants absorb and store carbon dioxide. So by planting more trees and creating more farms and by preserving the trees and plants that we already have, we can reduce the amount of carbon dioxide in the air.

Wind turbines spin to generate electricity that doesn't give off pollution or greenhouse gases. If people on Earth switch to using clean ways of producing energy, we may be able to slow or stop global warming.

In 1997 thirty-seven countries signed a treaty called the Kyoto Protocol (named for the city in Japan where the signing took place). The agreement took effect in 2005. The countries all agreed to burn less fossil fuel and reduce the amount of greenhouse gases they released into the atmosphere. Under the treaty, each nation must reduce greenhouse gas emissions by a certain percentage. Countries that stay under their emissions goals can sell "carbon credits" to nations that are having a hard time meeting their goals. These credits allow a purchasing nation to emit more greenhouse gases. Some Americans worry that burning less fossil fuel would restrict business and hurt the U.S. economy. Therefore, the United States has not signed the Kyoto Protocol.

Many insects thrive in warm weather, so global warming has allowed insects to live in places that were once too cold for them. Some of these insects can spread disease. For instance, some mosquitoes carry malaria, a deadly disease. Warmer weather is bringing mosquitoes—and malaria—to places where they haven't been seen before.

Global warming has a few positives. For instance, warmer temperatures will lead to longer growing seasons in some parts of the world. In cold places like Russia, northern China, and the U.S. Great Plains, farmers might be able to grow more food. But in most places, agriculture will suffer. Floods, droughts, and hurricanes will damage farmland and crops, potentially leading to mass starvation.

Does global warming signal the end of the world? Will it bring about the end of human society? Probably not. But global warming will certainly change human life as we know it. It will probably bring about homelessness, water shortages, food shortages, and disease. Some people predict that wars will increase, as people fight over scarce food, water, and other resources. Although global warming is not the end of the world, it is certainly something to worry about.

NUCLEAR WAR

Since the end of World War II, people have worried what a nuclear war—a war in which nuclear weapons are the main destructive force—might do to Earth. Even a small nuclear bomb is capable of destroying an entire city. In fact, the average nuclear bomb contains as much power as all bombs dropped during World War II combined.

A large nuclear war would be catastrophic to all life on Earth. The explosions themselves would destroy huge areas of land and kill millions of people. But even those not killed in the explosions would still be in danger. Nuclear explosions give off bursts of powerful radiation. This radiation can travel for miles

at nearly the speed of light. People dosed by the radiation would suffer serious burns and be at long-term risk of developing cancer.

In addition, nuclear explosions would throw about 500 million tons (453 million metric tons) of radioactive dust (dust containing radiation) high into Earth's atmosphere. Winds would carry the dust for hundreds or even thousands of miles. As it settled to the ground, the falling dust (called nuclear fallout) would contaminate anything it touched, including water and soil. The water would be unsafe to drink for years. The soil would also be contaminated. Plants that grew in the soil would be unsafe to eat.

This illustration shows a nuclear strike on Chicago, Illinois. But explosions alone would account for only part of the damage of a nuclear war. After the explosions, radioactive fallout and nuclear winter would destroy most life on Earth.

If the harm from a nuclear war were limited to the direct effects of the explosions and fallout, billions of people would die. But some people and other living things would survive. Life would still continue on Earth. However, the effects of a nuclear war would not be limited to the immediate effects of explosions and fallout. Earth's atmosphere is mostly made of nitrogen gas. Nuclear bombs exploding in the atmosphere would turn this nitrogen into nitrogen oxides. These chemicals would destroy the atmosphere's ozone layer, which protects us from the Sun's deadly ultraviolet radiation.

Meanwhile, human society would be thrown into chaos. The destruction of cities would mean the breakdown of government and health services. Telephones, computers, and other electrical devices would not work. Public transportation systems would shut down. With homes and buildings destroyed, most people wouldn't have shelter from the cold. Burning cities and forests, set on fire by exploding bombs, would pour smoke and poisonous gases into the atmosphere. But as bad as all that sounds, the situation would get even worse.

NUCLEAR WINTER

The radioactive dust thrown into the atmosphere by nuclear explosions would cause damage beyond just the death, cancer, and contamination caused by fallout. The tons of dust thrown high in the air would take months or even years to settle back to the surface. Up in the air, the dust would block sunlight. Without sunlight, Earth would grow dark.

With the dark would come cold. Within a few months or even less, temperatures all over the planet would drop below the freezing point (32°F, or 0°C). For a short time, Earth would get as cold as −13°F (−25°C). The darkness and cold would last for several months—a scenario known as nuclear winter.

Without sunlight, crops and other plants would die. People and animals would run out of food. Most of the humans and animals that had survived the nuclear bombing would begin to starve. Making matters worse, a constant shower of fine, radioactive dust would fall from the darkened skies. For people on the ground, the shower of radiation would be like getting tens of thousands of medical X-rays all at once. The radiation would sicken and kill millions of people.

Once the skies cleared, the problems wouldn't end. With the ozone layer destroyed, people would be exposed to ultraviolet radiation from the Sun. The UV rays would cause skin cancer and also damage people's immunity systems. As a result, disease would spread rapidly around the world. Meanwhile, few or no hospitals and health workers would be available to care for sick people.

MUTUALLY ASSURED DESTRUCTION

Of all the end-of-the-world scenarios, nuclear war is one of the most frightening. A nuclear war guarantees not only the death of most humans but also the destruction of almost all life on Earth.

Protesters demonstrate at a nuclear weapons plant in Oak Ridge, Tennessee. Many people want nations to stop building and stockpiling nuclear bombs.

Because of the horrors of nuclear war, many people think nuclear weapons should be outlawed and that existing nuclear weapons should be destroyed.

In 1945 the United States and the Soviet Union began the Cold War. The two powerful nations did not fight each other directly, but relations between them were tense and hostile. Both nations, as well as many of their allies, stockpiled nuclear weapons. Meanwhile, military experts put forth a doctrine called mutually assured destruction. The idea was that neither the United States, the Soviet Union, nor any other nation would dare use nuclear weapons. To do so would guarantee retaliation— with nuclear weapons. The resulting nuclear war would kill almost everyone on all sides of the conflict. In theory, this guaranteed destruction would dissuade any nation from using its nuclear weapons.

In 1991 the Soviet Union broke apart and the Cold War ended. But the end of the Cold War did not mean the end of the threat of nuclear war. Many nations around the world, including the United States, Russia (the largest state in the former Soviet Union), China, and North Korea—still have nuclear weapons. Other nations, such as Iran, are developing them. People also worry that terrorist groups might build or acquire nuclear weapons. Even a small-scale nuclear conflict, carried out with just a few bombs, would still lead to widespread destruction and death.

JAPAN 2011: MULTILEVEL DISASTER

On March 11, 2011, a powerful undersea earthquake struck near the northeastern coast of Honshu, the main island of Japan. The earthquake caused the floor of the Pacific Ocean to buckle. This motion created a huge tsunami, which spread rapidly in all directions. The giant wave measured more than 33 feet (9 m) high. When it hit the coast of Honshu, it destroyed everything in its path. It swept away people, cars, and even buildings.

The earthquake itself also did terrible damage. It knocked down houses and other buildings, burying people under rubble. Altogether, the earthquake and tsunami killed at least fifteen thousand people. The disaster left hundreds of thousands of Japanese people without homes.

But the disaster didn't end there. The earthquake damaged several Japanese nuclear reactors, or power plants. The damaged reactors released radiation into the surrounding air, water, and soil. In high levels, radiation can kill living things. It can cause diseases such as cancer. For safety, the Japanese government evacuated, or moved, people living near the damaged reactors. But it's hard to completely protect people and other living things from radiation. Radioactive (radiation-containing) particles can take thousands of years to become nonradioactive. And since wind and water can carry radiation from one place to another, it can be nearly impossible to keep radiation from spreading.

The disaster in Japan worried people all over the world. Many big cities, such as Los Angeles and San Francisco in the United States, are in earthquake zones. A big earthquake near one of these cities might do even more damage than the Japanese quake. In addition, around the world, many nuclear reactors are in earthquake zones. People hope to learn from the disaster in Japan to make nuclear reactors safer.

In this photo taken on March 16, 2011, smoke rises from the Fukushima Daiichi nuclear power generating plant reactor No. 3, which was damaged in the Japanese earthquake on March 11. Radiation from the leaking power plant was later found in Japan's food and water supply.

The influenza epidemic of 1918–1919 killed more people around the world than World War I (1914–1918). In this picture, flu patients are treated at a Kansas army hospital.

CHAPTER 6
THE END OF THE HUMAN SPECIES?

People are living things, and like all living things, we can die or be killed. Any number of events—nuclear war, a gamma-ray burst, or an asteroid strike—could kill great numbers of humans on Earth. But more likely killers are lurking all around us. These killers are bacteria and viruses that cause deadly diseases. A pandemic, or worldwide outbreak of disease, could potentially kill vast numbers of people.

Pandemics have happened before. In the 1300s, a disease called bubonic plague spread across Europe and other parts of Earth. The disease eventually killed one-third of Europe's people. In 1918 and 1919, a deadly form of flu spread rapidly around the world. It killed about 25 million people.

FROM DISEASE TO PANDEMIC

Many diseases, such as measles and smallpox, kill some people but not others. That's because, over time, humans have developed some immunity to these diseases. Immunity is a built-in protection that helps the body fight disease. Pandemics usually result from diseases for which humans have little or no immunity. For instance, sometimes a disease that commonly infects animals spreads to humans. Since the disease is new to the human species, people haven't built up any immunity to it. So the disease is more likely to kill the people who get it. Anthrax, Ebola fever, and swine flu are all diseases that can pass from animals to humans.

For a pandemic to occur, a disease must pass quickly from one person to another. If a disease spreads slowly, researchers will have time to develop protections against the disease, such as a vaccine (a preventive treatment, often given as a shot). A pandemic disease must also pass easily from one person to another. Some diseases spread when people cough or sneeze—which makes them easy to pass on. But to cause a pandemic, the disease can't kill its victims too quickly. If people die right away after getting the disease, they won't have time to infect others. Finally, for a disease to turn into a pandemic, it has to be resistant to medications. So it must be a disease for which there is no surefire vaccine, treatment, or cure.

People in San Francisco line up to receive a flu vaccine. If researchers can't develop a vaccine for a certain disease, it could lead to a pandemic.

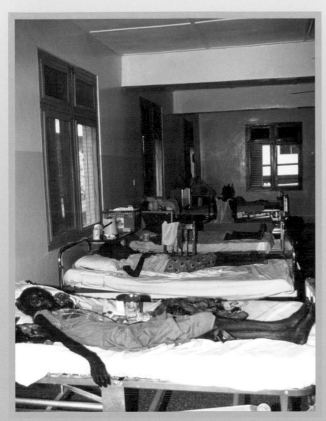

AIDS has reached epidemic levels in parts of Africa. These AIDS patients also have tuberculosis.

Acquired immunodeficiency syndrome (AIDS) has almost all the ingredients needed for a pandemic. The disease originated with chimpanzees and spread to humans, who had no immunity to it. The virus that causes the disease can easily pass from one person to another via blood, during sex, or even from mother to child at the time of birth.

AIDS doesn't kill people right away. In fact, people don't usually develop the disease until two to fifteen years after infection. Therefore, they might infect many others before they even know they're sick. Finally, there is no cure for AIDS, although scientists have developed treatments to slow the progress of the disease. In southern and central Africa, AIDS has reached epidemic levels. Almost twenty-five million people there have the disease. In 2009 nearly two million Africans died of AIDS.

SUPERBUG

Small organisms called bacteria can cause many kinds of diseases, such as pneumonia and tuberculosis. Doctors normally treat such diseases with antibiotics. These medicines can kill or stop the growth of bacteria. But bacteria can mutate, or change their genetic structure, very quickly. Sometimes an

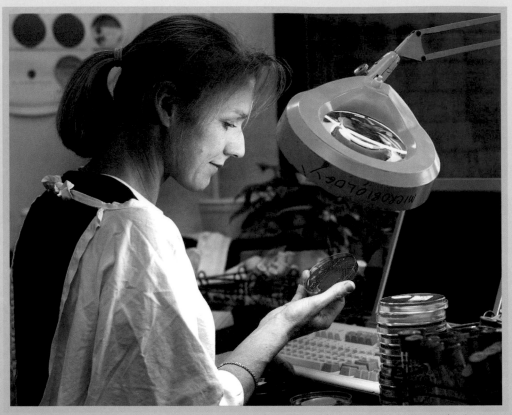

A researcher examines an antibiotic-resistant "superbug" in a laboratory. Bacteria that can resist antibiotics pose a serious threat to public health.

antibiotic works against a certain bacterium for a while. Then the bacterium mutates and becomes resistant to—or able to withstand—the antibiotic. The medicine no longer works.

In 2010 scientists discovered a kind of bacteria that is highly resistant to almost all antibiotics. Antibiotics destroy bacteria by reacting with the membrane, or skin, that surrounds the organism. The membrane of this new kind of bacteria is not affected by antibiotics. And this type of resistance is spreading through many different kinds of bacteria. Public health officials worry that such superbugs will spread quickly through the human population, causing a pandemic.

Tuberculosis is a deadly lung disease caused by a bacterium. Doctors normally treat tuberculosis with antibiotics. But a new form of the disease, XDR-TB, appears to be a superbug. This version of tuberculosis is highly resistant to antibiotics and appears to be spreading worldwide. More than forty thousand new cases are reported each year. Many scientists and doctors fear that XDR-TB will become the next pandemic.

MAD SCIENTISTS

Most diseases spread naturally. But people can also spread disease deliberately. In ancient times, armies sometimes threw human and animal waste into enemy cities and fortifications. The waste carried disease, which then spread among the enemy population. Armies used dead bodies the same way, hurling them into enemy territory to spread disease. In the American colonies in the 1700s, one British general deliberately gave smallpox-infected blankets to enemy Indians. The Indians had no immunity to smallpox and quickly caught the disease.

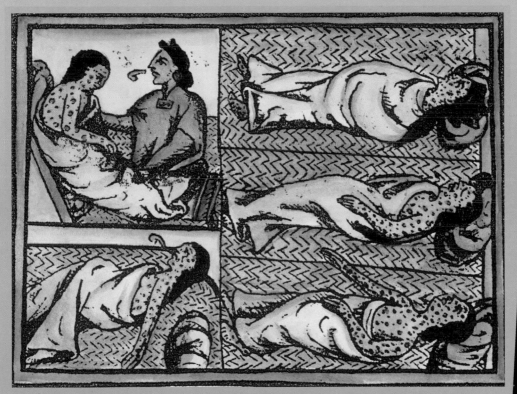

This sixteenth-century illustration shows Aztec people dying from smallpox in Mexico. European explorers and settlers brought the disease to the Americas and sometimes spread it deliberately to Indian peoples.

In the twentieth century, during World War I (1914–1918), World War II, and the Cold War, many governments studied, tested, and stockpiled biological weapons (disease-carrying weapons), although they were rarely used.

Using biological weapons against an enemy is called biowarfare. In modern times, people also worry about bioterrorism. They fear that terrorist groups will carry out small-scale attacks with biological weapons, spreading diseases to large numbers of people. The situation is not unknown. In 1984 in the state of Oregon, members of a religious cult deliberately infected food in nearby restaurants and grocery stores. More than 750 people fell ill. In 1993 another religious cult tried to spread anthrax and botulism in Tokyo, Japan, but the attempt failed. In 2001 someone mailed envelopes containing anthrax spores to U.S. politicians and journalists. Twenty-two people were infected and five died. None of these attacks caused a widespread outbreak of disease. But the threat of bioterrorism is real. In fact, when the United States invaded Iraq in 2003, U.S. leaders said they were worried that Iraq was developing biological weapons.

Letter to Tom Brokaw

These envelopes, addressed to a newscaster and a U.S. senator in 2001, contained anthrax spores.

SURVIVALISTS PLAN FOR THE END

People have been preparing for the end of the world, in one form or another, for hundreds of years. In the years leading up to A.D. 1000, believing that Judgment Day was at hand, some people prepared by devoting their lives to God. More recently, during the Cold War, some Americans built bomb shelters in their backyards *(diagram below).*

These were concrete structures designed to protect people from nuclear explosions and radioactive fallout. People stocked the shelters with canned goods, water, and other supplies they would need after a nuclear war.

In the twenty-first century, a new survivalist movement has emerged. Convinced that human civilization

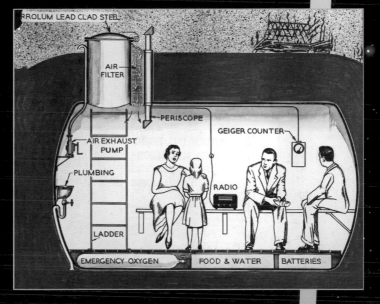

is breaking down, many people are preparing to live off the land. Some have moved to the wilderness, where they survive by killing wild animals and collecting edible wild plants. Some survivalists build their own shelters, gather rainwater for drinking and washing, and grow their own food. They live "off the grid"—that is, with no connections to gas or electric lines or piped-in water systems. Hundreds of books, TV shows, and websites are dedicated to teaching people how to survive without the comforts of grocery stores, cars, or hot running water. Lots of businesses cater to survivalists. They sell water purification equipment, bulk food supplies, seeds, farming equipment, and guns and ammunition. Survivalists want to be prepared for anything: nuclear war, bioterrorism, natural disasters, and pandemics.

THE NEXT PANDEMIC?

In the twenty-first century, diseases can spread quickly. That's because people can travel quickly by airplane from one part of the world to another. With modern transportation, a new disease might spread across a large area before medical researchers can find a vaccine, a cure, or a treatment. If symptoms don't show up until long after infection, as is the case with AIDS, a disease might spread around the world before researchers even know about it.

What would happen at the first signs of a pandemic? The first order of business would be to contain the disease—that is, to keep it from spreading further. Government officials might place restrictions on long-distance travel. They might quarantine, or isolate, people who already had the disease. They would close public facilities such as schools. They would tell people to avoid crowds or close contact with others. Medical researchers would begin looking for a treatment for the disease.

But if the disease was especially deadly, quick-spreading, or untreatable, people might panic. They might flood to hospitals and health clinics in search of help. Hospitals and health workers would be overwhelmed. Fearing for their own lives, some health workers might not report to work. Other people would be afraid to leave their homes, so they wouldn't go to work either. Businesses would shut down. Stores would run out of food. As the death toll climbed, businesses that care for the dead—morgues, funeral homes, and cemeteries—wouldn't be able to keep up. Dead bodies might lie unattended. People would be buried in mass graves.

This scenario is unlikely, but it's not impossible. The United States and other rich nations have well-functioning public health systems. Police officers, hospital workers, government officials, and others are trained to deal with health emergencies. But in poor nations, such systems are not as well developed. If a pandemic were to develop, it might do the most damage among poor people.

POPULATION REBOUND

Would a pandemic kill everyone on Earth—wiping out the entire human species? It's unlikely. Even the most deadly viruses and bacteria don't kill everyone they infect. A certain portion of the human population would probably survive a pandemic, no matter how deadly. Although the population might be greatly decreased after a pandemic, the survivors would have new children and the population would again start to increase.

Similarly, warfare and natural disasters can kill thousands—even millions—of people. But they never come close to wiping out the entire human species. For instance, World War II was one of the most destructive wars in human history. Perhaps as many as 70 million people—soldiers and civilians—lost their lives because of the war. When a tsunami struck Southeast Asia in 2004, the toll of death and destruction was tremendous. More than 150,000 people died. The 2010 earthquake that hit Haiti killed more than 200,000 people. And in 2011, more than 15,000 people died in an earthquake and subsequent tsunami that struck Japan. But none of these events wiped out the human race.

A tsunami slams into Phuket, Thailand, in December 2004. The disaster killed more than 150,000 people—yet that is a tiny fraction of the world population.

Nobel Peace Prize winner Wangari Maathai of Kenya *(left)* and Norwegian prime minister Jens Stoltenberg *(right)* shake hands as they celebrate the opening of the Svalbard Global Seed Vault in Norway in 2008. The black box is the first of many sealed cases containing seeds to be stored in the seed bank.

BANKING AGAINST DISASTER

Scientists have already created hundreds of seed banks. These are special storage areas where plant seeds can be kept safely. The hope is that people can use the seeds after a global disaster to grow food they need to survive.

The seed banks contain millions of seeds from thousands of different kinds of plants. If stored under the right conditions, seeds can survive for hundreds and even thousands of years. For instance, in 2005 scientists grew a date palm tree from a two-thousand-year-old seed found in Israel.

One of the world's largest seed banks opened in 2008. It is the Svalbard Global Seed Vault in Norway. It is built inside a mountain on the island of Spitsbergen, about 800 miles (1,300 km) from the North Pole. It is designed to survive the bomb blasts and radiation of a global nuclear war. The permanently frozen soil on Spitsbergen helps keep the underground vault cold. Just as keeping food in your refrigerator helps make it last longer, keeping seeds cold helps preserve them. In addition, seeds are protected by 3-foot-thick (1 m) walls of steel-reinforced concrete. The vault is sealed by two giant, blast-proof doors.

In addition to seed banks, humans might someday create gigantic gene banks. These banks would store the genes of tens of thousands of species of plants and animals. After a life-destroying disaster, such as a gamma-ray burst, people could use the genes to grow new plants and animals. The banks might even store human genes, so we could create new people after a disaster.

In fact, the human population continues to increase steadily. In 2011 the population stood at about 6.9 billion. Social scientists think the population will reach 9 billion by 2050. So we certainly don't have to worry about the human species dying out in the near future. However, we do have to worry how Earth will be able to support so many people. Will there be enough food and clean water to support 9 billion humans? Will we have enough fuel for cooking and keeping warm? Will people go to war over scarce resources? Will the foundations of government and society break down?

Perhaps the human species is too successful and too resilient. As the population grows and grows, chaos might be the result. It won't be the end of the world in terms of the death of humankind, but it certainly might be the end of life as we know it.

EXTINCTION AND EVOLUTION

Over millions of years, plant and animal species have come and gone on Earth. Some species have become extinct. That is, they have died out altogether. Some died because the climate became too hot or too cold for them to survive. Others could not find enough food and died out. Still others were hunted to extinction by humans. Dinosaurs became extinct because of the asteroid strike in the Yucatán millions of years ago.

Other species did not exactly die out—they simply changed. They adapted to changes in their environment and evolved into new kinds of plants and animals. A British naturalist named Charles Darwin published his theory of evolution in 1859. Darwin explained how plants and animals pass on useful qualities from generation to generation, while harmful traits are not passed on. For instance, in a place where most food plants grow high on trees, an animal with a long neck has an advantage over those with shorter necks. The animal can more easily reach up and get food. Therefore, it is more likely to survive than animals with short necks. It will pass its traits—such as its long neck—to later generations. Creatures with less useful characteristics, such as short necks, will be less likely to get food and survive and therefore will be less likely to pass on their traits. Over time, a new species might evolve—an animal with a very long neck. And the older, shorter-necked species might die out.

Charles Darwin explained how living things evolve in response to changes in the environment. As our world changes in the future, humans might evolve into an entirely new species.

BECOMING SOMETHING DIFFERENT

As with other living things, it's also possible that humans could evolve into a new kind of animal. We would not disappear from Earth, but we might become something completely different. Our species, *Homo sapiens*, would no longer exist. A more successful species would take our place.

What might that species be like? Many scientists have wondered about that. The topic is a favorite of science-fiction writers. Evolution responds to pressures from the environment, so human evolution will depend on what kinds of changes take place on Earth. Will Earth become hotter or colder? Will the atmosphere change? Each different change would set human evolution on a different course. Perhaps our jaws will change due to eating new kinds of food. Perhaps, because of typing on computer and cell phone keyboards, our fingers will change.

Someday, scientists might even create new kinds of humans

in the laboratory. They would use genetic engineering. That is, they would rearrange genes—the basic building blocks of life—to create new, different life-forms. Scientists have already used genetic engineering to create new versions of plants and animals. For instance, they have created insect-resistant crops and fish that grow extremely quickly. In the future, scientists might be able to engineer humans who can withstand changes in Earth's climate or who require less food for survival.

In 1927 a science-fiction writer imagined that in the future, humans would turn into "machine men," with enormous brains and small, weak bodies.

This illustration shows how the Moon was created. A huge asteroid struck Earth and blasted away big chunks of our planet. The material that blasted off into space became the Moon.

CHAPTER 7
THE END OF EARTH

Destroying life on our planet is a lot easier than destroying the planet itself. All the plants and animals on Earth combined weigh about 75 billion tons (68 billion metric tons). This sounds like a lot, but it's nothing compared to Earth itself, which weighs about 6.6 sextillion tons (6 sextillion metric tons). That's 6.6 with twenty zeroes following it. This means that all life on our planet combined is only about 0.00000000126 percent the weight of Earth as a whole. It would take a lot of force to destroy anything as big and massive as our planet.

A MEETING WITH THEIA

The destruction of Earth did nearly happen billions of years ago, when the solar system was still young. The Sun and the planets had just formed out of a giant cloud of gas and dust. In addition to the planets, the solar system contained thousands of meteoroids and asteroids. Large and small, made of rock, metal, and ice, these bodies zipped every which way through the solar system. When one of these objects hit a planet or a moon, it left a crater on its surface.

Some of these bodies were nearly as large as the planets themselves. One was a planet-sized asteroid named Theia. It was almost as big as Mars. Scientists believe that about 4.6 billion years ago, Theia crashed into Earth. The collision nearly destroyed Earth. Earth's outer layers peeled away like the skin of an orange. The whole Earth became molten from the heat created by the impact.

LEAVING EARTH

Russian astronomer Konstantin Tsiolkovsky (1857-1935) once said: "The Earth is the cradle of humanity, but mankind cannot stay in the cradle forever." Tsiolkovsky meant that people would someday have to leave Earth to live somewhere else in the solar system. Certainly, a colony, or human settlement, somewhere in space would come in handy if a global disaster were ever to destroy Earth.

Where could people go? Scientists are exploring several possibilities. One is the Moon. At 240,000 miles (386,000 km) from Earth, it is the closest of all the bodies in the solar system. In the 1960s and the 1970s, U.S. astronauts traveled to the Moon and back in just three days. The Moon would be a hostile place to live, though. Because it spins slowly on its axis, its days and nights are each two weeks long. Temperatures can get up to 225°F (107°C) during the day and plummet to -243°F (-153°C) at night. The Moon has no atmosphere or magnetic field to protect its surface from meteorites or radiation. If people were to set up colonies on the Moon, they would have to live underground. They would have to bring in their own air, water, and food.

Mars would be the next best choice for human settlement. Although it is only one-third the size of Earth, it is the most Earthlike of all the planets. Mars has an atmosphere and water, although most of the water is underground and frozen. Its days are almost exactly as long as Earth's. But Mars is a cold world. The average temperature is -55°F (-50°C). And people could not breathe on Mars because the atmosphere doesn't have enough oxygen. To live on Mars, people would need to live in airtight shelters. They would need to extract oxygen from the ice that lies buried deep under the Martian surface. This same ice would also provide water for the colonists. Eventually, people might be able to heat, alter, and thicken Mars's atmosphere, so they could breathe the air and move around outdoors.

A third possibility is to build our own worlds in outer space. These would be giant, artificial planets capable of holding thousands and perhaps millions of people. Supplies could be regularly shipped in from Earth. But if Earth had been destroyed, a space colony would have to be completely self-sustaining. It would have to generate its own power and air. Colonists would have to raise their own food. They would have to recycle water over and over again or ship in water from other parts of the solar system.

In the 1960s, U.S. aircraft engineer Darrell Romick designed a huge space station that would orbit Earth and serve as a home to twenty thousand people. In the 1970s, U.S. physicist Gerard K. O'Neill designed a space colony that could house up to ten million people. His structure was a huge cylinder 5 miles (8 km) wide and 20 miles (32 km) long. No one has ever acted on these plans, however. As it stands, the cost of building a space colony is too high, and the challenges of transporting and housing large numbers of people in space are too great. The closest we have is the International Space Station, which is home to just a few astronauts at a time. But perhaps future humans will figure out how to solve the challenges of space colonization. So if and when the end of the world does come, people will have another home to go to.

These illustrations show what human settlements might look like at a Moon base *(top)*, a Mars base *(middle)*, and in space cities *(bottom)*.

The collision threw a vast amount of material from both Earth and Theia—rocks, dust, and other debris—out into space. This material formed a ring around Earth. Then gravitational pull between the separate pieces of debris caused them to come together. They fused together to form the Moon. (Theia is still with us. During the collision with Earth, the core of the asteroid merged with Earth's core. It is still there, 4,000 miles (6,400 km) beneath your feet.)

COULD IT HAPPEN AGAIN?

What would happen if another planet-sized asteroid hit Earth? It would probably once again turn Earth into molten rock and would certainly wipe out all life. But lucky for us, asteroids as big as Theia are no longer zipping through the solar system.

A collision like the one that created our Moon would be a devastating disaster. It would destroy all life on our planet.

Millions of years ago, the gravity of the Sun and planets attracted most of these asteroids. The biggest planet, Jupiter, was very good at pulling in stray asteroids, because its gravity is so strong. It acted like a giant vacuum cleaner, sweeping the solar system clean of extra rock, metal, and ice. The only asteroids remaining in the solar system are not big enough to do as much damage to Earth as Theia did.

PLANET ON PLANET

Even the collision with Theia didn't destroy Earth completely. For Earth to actually break apart, it would have to run into something at least 60 percent as massive as itself. Mars has only 11 percent the mass (amount of material) of Earth, so it wouldn't do the job. Venus, with 81 percent the mass of Earth, is often called Earth's twin because the planets are close in size. It would destroy Earth if the two planets were to collide. So would any of the larger planets, such as Jupiter, Saturn, Uranus, or Neptune. However, a planet cannot suddenly leave its orbit and run into another one. The gravity that holds planets in orbit is too powerful. So we have nothing to fear from another planet in our solar system.

What about a planet hitting Earth from outside the solar system? This is possible. Astronomers have identified "rogue planets." These are planets that move through space on their own. They do not orbit stars. Even so, the chances of one of these planets traveling into the solar system and running into Earth are extremely low.

DEATH BY BLACK HOLE

All stars eventually die. When some massive stars—giants and supergiants—reach the end of their lives, they collapse. As a giant or supergiant collapses, it becomes denser. So its material is squeezed into a smaller space than it once occupied. As the

If a black hole came anywhere near Earth, our planet would be doomed. Earth *(foreground)* would be torn to pieces and sucked into the black hole *(background)*.

star become denser, its gravity increases. The increased gravity causes the star to collapse even more. It becomes smaller and smaller and ever denser—until it becomes a black hole.

A black hole's gravity is extremely strong. Anything that falls within its gravitational field cannot escape. With their extraordinary gravity, black holes absorb nearby space objects, such as dust, meteorites, and asteroids. The largest black holes can swallow entire stars. Nothing, not even light, can escape from a black hole. For this reason, black holes are invisible. Scientists find them by looking for two different things. One is the pull that their tremendous gravity has on nearby bodies, such as stars. Scientists also look for signs of the huge amounts of energy released when matter falls into a black hole.

If a black hole were to enter our solar system, scientists would be aware of the effects long before it got anywhere near Earth. The black hole's powerful gravity would tug at the planets and disturb their orbits. As the black hole approached Earth, it would tear the planet into little pieces. The shredded Earth would then join a disk of gas and dust surrounding the black hole. Eventually, the remains of Earth would spiral into the black hole and be lost forever.

Little could be done to prevent a collision with an approaching black hole. But such an event is extremely unlikely anyway. There are no black holes nearby. The one closest to our solar system is 1,600 light-years away.

As the Sun grows larger and hotter over time, Earth's oceans will dry up.

CHAPTER 8
GOING, GOING, GONE

No matter what happens on Earth or what happens in outer space, Earth is inevitably doomed. That's because the Sun won't stay the same forever. Like a human being, it will grow old and eventually die. In about 1.1 billion years, the Sun will begin to change. It will grow a lot brighter and hotter. This extra heat will have a devastating effect on Earth. The average surface temperature of Earth will rise from about 68°F (20°C) to 167°F (75°C). Earth's oceans will evaporate. All plants and animals will die. The planet will become a stark, lifeless desert. If the human race hasn't ended before then or if people haven't figured out how to leave Earth and live someplace else, it will surely end at this point.

Over the following 700 million years, the Sun won't grow any brighter. But it will grow larger. Eventually the Sun will swell to one and a half times its present size and will become more than twice as bright. Then it will cool down a little. From the parched surface of Earth, if people were still around to see it, the Sun would look like an enormous orange ball hanging in a misty sky.

About one billion years after that, the Sun will lose more than one-quarter of the mass of its outer surface. It will blow this material off into space in a series of explosions. A less massive Sun will have less gravity. And with less gravity to attract them, the planets will move farther from the Sun. Venus will become as far from the Sun as Earth is now. Earth will also move farther away.

Eventually, in about five billion years, the ever-swelling Sun will become a star called a red giant. It will be 166 times larger than the Sun we know. This is almost as large as the circle traced by Earth as it orbits the Sun in the twenty-first century. The flames of the giant Sun will devour the planets Mercury and Venus. The mountains of Earth will melt and flow like red-hot molasses into vast seas of lava. A bloated red Sun will fill more than half the sky.

Five billion years from now, the Sun will become a red giant star *(left)*. It will balloon to many times its present size. The tremendous heat will boil away Earth's oceans and melt much of its surface. Eventually, the Sun will use up all its fuel *(right)*. All that will remain of the Sun will be a tiny white dwarf star. Earth will be a cold, lifeless planet.

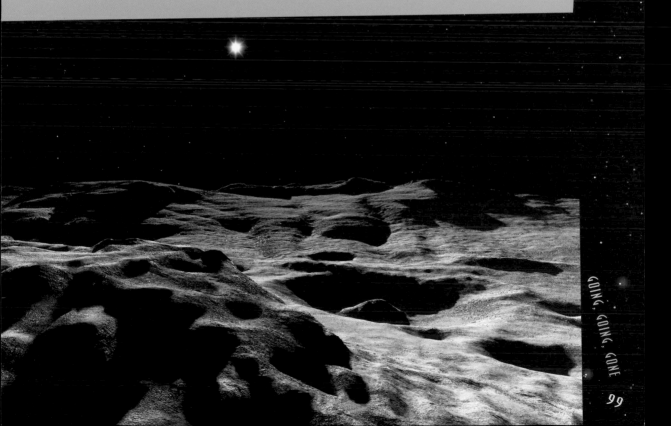

After the Sun reaches its maximum size as a red giant, it will begin to shrink, though it will never get less than ten times its present size. Nothing much will happen for the next 110 million years.

Then, again, the Sun will swell until it doubles its size, but by then, it will be nearly out of the hydrogen and helium it uses for fuel. Next, huge portions of its atmosphere will blow off into space, until nearly half of its mass is lost. The loss of mass will cause another reduction in gravity. Earth—by then little more than a burned-out cinder—will move even farther away.

The Sun will begin to pulse violently, like the light on top of a police car. Every time it pulses, it will lose more mass. A final pulse will blow away the last of the Sun's outer surface. All that will remain will be its bare core of heavy elements, such as iron. It will be a solid sphere about the size of Earth.

The remains of the Sun will be extremely hot, but this heat will be residual, or left over from when the Sun was shining. Nothing will replace the heat as the Sun cools. It will be like a hot coal in a barbecue grill. It will slowly cool until eventually it too becomes a cold, dark cinder.

EDWIN HUBBLE AND THE EXPANDING UNIVERSE

Edwin Hubble

U.S. astronomer Edwin Hubble (1889–1953) made a startling discovery in the 1920s. As he studied distant galaxies, he found that no matter which way he looked into space, all the galaxies appeared to be moving away from our own. Moreover, the farther away a galaxy was, the faster it was moving away from us. There could be only one explanation: the universe is growing larger. It is expanding.

Hubble realized that if the universe is expanding and all the galaxies are moving farther and farther apart, there must have been a time in the distant past when the galaxies were much closer together. In fact, there must have been a time when all the matter in the universe was crowded into a very small space. This idea was the origin of the big bang theory.

GOOD-BYE, MILKY WAY

After the Sun starts to grow bigger and hotter, people and other life on Earth will certainly die. So unless we've figured out how to live elsewhere in space by then, we won't be around to see the next big change—when our own Milky Way galaxy comes to an end.

All the stars we can see in the sky are part of the Milky Way. The Milky Way is a spiral galaxy—a vast collection of 200 to 400 billion stars, swirling together like cream stirred into a cup of hot coffee. The Milky Way is huge. It spans 100,000 light-years from edge to edge. This means that even if you could travel at the speed of light—186,000 miles (300,000 km) per second—it would take one hundred thousand years to make the trip from one side of the galaxy to the other.

The universe has between 100 billion and 200 billion galaxies. Although hundreds and even millions of light-years separate them, galaxies do sometimes run into one another. Is there any danger of the Milky Way running into another galaxy? Yes. In fact, a collision is certain. The Milky Way's nearest galactic neighbor is the Andromeda galaxy. It is almost a twin of our own galaxy. It lies about 2 million light-years away and can be seen in the night sky with a pair of binoculars. Our galaxy and Andromeda are headed toward each other at about 268,000 miles (431,000 km) per hour.

Astronomers think that in about two billion years, Andromeda will hit the Milky Way. The gravity from the galaxies will pull at each other's stars, distorting the galaxies into new shapes. The cores of the galaxies will orbit each other for another three billion years. During this time, they will collide at least one more time. Then they will finally merge into a single, gigantic, football-

When the Milky Way and Andromeda galaxies collide, as astronomers believe they will, the Sun might be thrown out of the galaxy entirely. This illustration shows what the colliding galaxies might look like from Earth—if the planet even exists by then.

COLLISION COURSE

The Milky Way is already colliding with another galaxy. Astronomers have observed the Milky Way absorbing a small galaxy called Canis Major. Canis Major is a midget compared to the Milky Way. The Milky Way's gravity has already torn the small galaxy into long, graceful loops and streams of stars.

shaped galaxy. Astronomers have dubbed this yet-to-be-created galaxy Milkomeda.

What will happen to the Sun and especially Earth as the two galaxies meet and merge? Astronomers' best guess is that the solar system will be swept into a wispy new arm of Milkomeda. Our Sun will probably be a red

This image, taken with cameras aboard the Hubble Space Telescope, shows two galaxies colliding.

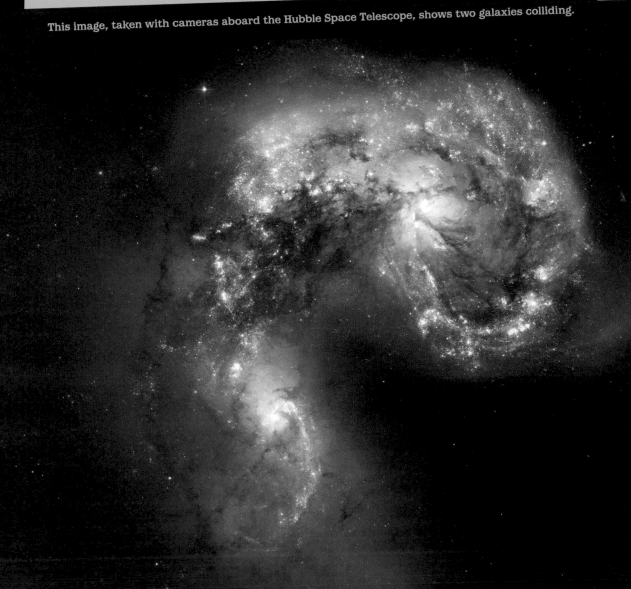

giant by then, and it will almost certainly survive the merger. That's because the galaxies will collide, but most of the stars in them won't. Galaxies are mostly empty space. The colliding galaxies would slip through each other like two drill teams marching at halftime during a football game. The chances of another star colliding with the Sun during this event are extremely slim. Any planets that are still orbiting the Sun at this time would also survive.

Although stars won't collide during the merger, the gas and dust between the stars will collide. These collisions will probably trigger a flurry of star formation. So instead of causing the deaths of stars, the collision of the two galaxies will result in the birth of hundreds of new ones.

While the Sun will probably escape the collision unharmed, there is a faint possibility that gravity from the collision could throw the Sun out of the galaxy entirely. This wouldn't much affect either the Sun or the planets still orbiting the Sun. But the night sky would be very different after that. If people were still around to see it, the night sky would be black and virtually starless.

THE END OF THE UNIVERSE

Almost 14 billion years ago, an incredible event took place. It was a giant explosion in which *everything*—matter (material), energy, time, and even space itself—began. Everything erupted from a single point. Scientists call this titanic explosion the big bang. It is not correct to imagine an empty space into which all matter and energy suddenly burst, because there was no space before the big bang. Space was created right along with matter, time, and everything else.

Ever since the big bang, the universe has been expanding. It continues to expand, with everything in the universe gradually moving farther away from everything else. The universe is also becoming cooler as it expands. At the moment of the big bang,

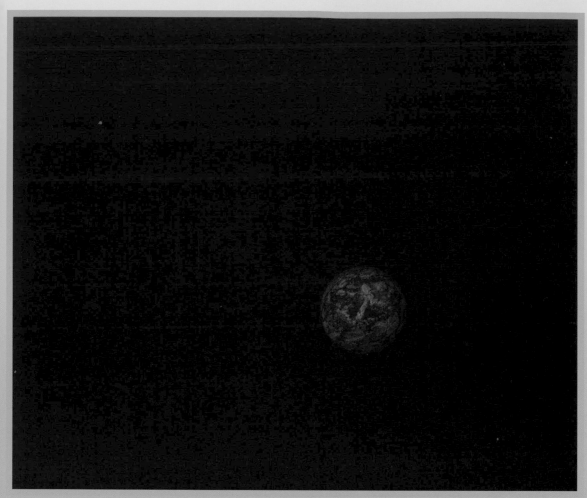

When all the energy in the universe is used up, only darkness and cold will remain.

the temperature of the universe was an incredible 180,000,000,
000,000,000,000,000,000,000,000°F (82,000,000,000,000,000,
000,000,000,000,000°C). In the twenty-first century, 13.7 billion
years later, the average temperature of the universe is a chilly
−454°F, or −270°C.

A BIG CRUNCH?

What will become of the universe in the distant future? Will it
continue to expand and cool? Will the expansion finally come
to a stop? Some scientists think the universe might start to
collapse back on itself, in the same way a ball tossed into the
air will inevitably slow down, stop, and then fall back to Earth.

If this were to happen, the universe would contract (shrink) slowly at first. Then, faster and faster, the galaxies would come closer together. Eventually, the universe would no longer be large enough for separate galaxies or stars. Everything would merge, like snowflakes compressed into a solid snowball. As the universe shrank, its temperature would increase tremendously. Finally, at the end, the universe would exist as it was at the beginning: as an infinitely small, infinitely dense, and infinitely hot point. Scientists call this scenario the big crunch.

After the big crunch, would the infinitely small point eventually explode again in another big bang, creating a brand-new universe? Have there been other big bangs, other big crunches, and other universes before our own? No one knows.

ONE-WAY TICKET

Most astronomers believe that the universe will keep on expanding forever rather than reversing course and shrinking. In this scenario, the distances between galaxies will grow greater and greater. All the galaxies around our own will eventually disappear into the unimaginable distance. In every galaxy, the stars will gradually burn out. No new stars will be born because the dust and gas needed to make new stars will be spread apart too thinly through space. The universe will slowly grow dimmer and colder.

Eventually, all the energy in the universe will be used up. Chemical reactions, including those that make life, intelligence, and thought possible, will cease. By then, perhaps 1,000 billion years in the future, nothing will be left of the universe but darkness, emptiness, and absolute cold. It will be the big freeze.

EPILOGUE

Most fact-based world-ending disasters are thousands, millions, and even billions of years in the future. They will not impact our lives or those of our children or their children. But it is important for us to think about things happening on Earth right now—things that directly affect the quality of life on this planet and things that we can do something about.

One example is nuclear war. If people were to use nuclear weapons, the results would certainly be catastrophic. A nuclear war would probably kill billions of people and most of the rest of the life on Earth. That is something to worry about—and it is something we can prevent. You can help prevent nuclear war by protesting against nuclear weapons, writing to your elected officials, and joining groups working to outlaw and destroy nuclear weapons around the world.

Global warming is another real danger that we can work against. Because much of global warming is caused by human activity, humans should be able to slow or stop it. It wouldn't be that hard. By decreasing the amount of greenhouse gases that get into the atmosphere, we can lessen the dangers of global warming. Since the main greenhouse gas is carbon dioxide, we need to produce as little of it as we can. There are a lot of ways to do that. You can do your part.

Most of the electricity we use comes from burning coal, and the burning of coal releases carbon dioxide into the atmosphere. So we can cut carbon dioxide emissions by using less electricity. You can help by turning off lights, your television, and your computer when you are not using them. Cars produce a lot of carbon dioxide, so the less we use cars, the better. Rather than asking your parents to drive you places, try walking or riding your bike instead. Take a bus or a train if possible. Adults can save energy by carpooling. For example, four people can ride together in one car instead of driving four cars to work.

Trees and other plants absorb carbon dioxide from the air. In the process, plants release oxygen, and people need oxygen to breathe. So you can help reduce carbon dioxide and produce

Lots of young people are working to protect Earth. Some protest nuclear weapons. Others plant trees and gardens to fight global warming.

more oxygen by planting trees and gardens. Planting is fun, it makes Earth look nicer, and it's a great way to reduce greenhouse gases.

You can help reduce pollution by recycling metal, glass, and plastic containers. The more we reuse old containers, the fewer containers will end up in landfills. Buy products that don't come wrapped in layers and layers of plastic, since most plastic packaging can't be recycled. Take your own reusable bags to the grocery store. When you are working in your garage or garden, don't let oils, fertilizers, paints, or detergents wash onto the ground or into drains. These steps are simple and if everyone followed them, Earth would be a cleaner place.

HIGH HOPES

It's easy to get discouraged when we think about all the ways the world could end. But remember, people are great inventors and problem solvers. We've sent spacecraft to other planets. We've invented computers, cell phones, and satellites. Who's to say we won't also create technology to save the world from disaster? Who's to say we won't figure out how to leave Earth and live in new worlds? Since most end-of-the-world scenarios are a long time in the future, we've got a lot of time to think and plan.

TIMELINE

ca. 14 billion B.C. The universe is created from a single point in an explosion and expansion called the big bang.

ca. 4.6 billion B.C. An asteroid called Theia crashes into Earth. The collision sends pieces of material from Earth and Theia hurling into space. The material eventually becomes the Moon.

ca. 440 million B.C. A mass extilting devastation wipes out most life on Earth, including dinosaurs.

ca. A.D. 95 A writer in the Middle East creates the Bible's Book of Revelation, which describes the Apocalypse, or end of the world in Christian teaching.

999 Some Christians prepare for the end of the world, which they believe will come in the year 1000.

1300s Bubonic plague kills about one-third of Europe's population.

1859 The Carrington Flare, a massive solar flare, disrupts electrical systems and causes auroras in skies all over Earth.

1908 A small asteroid or large meteoroid explodes over Siberia, knocking down trees and houses and killing reindeer.

1918–1919 A flu pandemic kills 25 million people around the globe.

1932	Astronomers discover the first of more than 260 asteroids that cross Earth's orbit.
1945	The United States drops nuclear bombs on two Japanese cities, killing tens of thousands of people and bringing an end to World War II.
1975-1995	A series of U.S. writers, using Mayan mythology and pseudoscience, predict that the world will end in 2012.
2005	A solar flare disrupts the worldwide Global Positioning System.
2008	The Svalbard Global Seed Vault opens in Norway. It is designed to preserve seeds in the event of a global catastrophe.
2009	Asteroids explode over Indonesia and Utah, but they do no damage.
2010	Two small asteroids pass less than 120,000 miles (193,000 km) from Earth. Scientists discover a "superbug" that is resistant to almost all antibiotics.
2011	A giant undersea earthquake strikes off the coast of Japan, killing at least fifteen thousand people. The quake causes a powerful tsunami and damages Japanese nuclear reactors. The world does not end on May 21, as predicted by some Christian believers.

GLOSSARY

Apocalypse: the end of the world, especially as described in the Book of Revelations

Armageddon: as described in Christian teachings, a battle between God and the devil leading up to Judgment Day and the end of the world

asteroid: a small, rocky or metallic body orbiting the Sun

astronomer: a scientist who studies outer space

atmosphere: the layer of gases surrounding a planet

big bang: a theory that says the universe began with an explosion from an infinitely hot, infinitely dense, infinitely tiny point. The theory is based on the research of U.S. astronomer Edwin Hubble.

black hole: a region of space whose gravity is so strong that nothing, not even light, can escape from it. Black holes form from massive stars that collapse.

drought: a long period of little or no rainfall

earthquake: a shaking or trembling of Earth, usually caused by movement of the plates that make up Earth's crust

epidemic: a widespread outbreak of disease. An epidemic that affects people all over Earth is called a pandemic.

evolution: the process by which plants and animals change over time by passing on useful genetic traits to future generations. These are often traits that help the plant or animal survive.

extinction: the dying out of an entire plant or animal species

fallout: radioactive particles that move through the atmosphere after a nuclear explosion

genetic engineering: cutting up and rejoining genes from a plant or an animal to create a different kind of organism

global warming: an increase in a planet's average temperature caused by a buildup of greenhouse gases in the atmosphere. Greenhouse gases trap the Sun's energy near Earth, keeping it from traveling back out into space.

gravity: a naturally occurring force that causes all massive objects, such as planets, moons, and stars, to pull on one another

greenhouse effect: the process by which heat from the Sun is captured beneath the atmosphere and cannot travel back into space

immunity: built-in protection against disease

magnetic field: a field of force around an electrically charged object (such as a magnet). A magnetic field surrounds Earth.

magnetic pole: one of the two ends of a magnet, usually designated as the north pole or the south pole. Earth has magnetic north and south poles.

orbit: to travel around another object in space; the path an object takes through space as it travels around another body

ozone layer: a layer of ozone (a form of oxygen) high in Earth's atmosphere that protects Earth from ultraviolet radiation from the Sun

pandemic: an outbreak of disease that affects people worldwide

prophecy: a prediction of something to come

pseudoscience: scientific theories that are not supported by accepted scientific methodology

radiation: energy given off in the form of waves or small particles of matter. Some types of radiation, such as gamma rays and ultraviolet rays, can be deadly.

satellites: human-made spacecraft that orbit Earth. Instruments aboard spacecraft help people study the solar system and the universe, monitor weather, navigate, and communicate.

solar flare: a sudden, gigantic explosion of energy and mass from the Sun

solar wind: a stream of electromagnetic particles emitted by the Sun

sunspot: a magnetic whirlpool on the surface of the Sun

tsunami: a giant ocean wave created by an earthquake or an undersea volcano

ultraviolet light: an invisible form of light given off by the Sun or by lightning or another electrical spark in the air. Ultraviolet light can cause sunburn, skin cancer, and other health problems.

vaccine: a bacteria or a virus that has been killed or weakened. When injected, vaccines trigger the body to create immunity against certain diseases.

water vapor: water in gas form

SOURCE NOTES

27 2012hoax, "Debunking the 2012 Doomsday," 2012hoax, n.d., http://www.2012hoax.org (February 5, 2011).

29 "The End of the World Part 1—Polar Shift, an Earth Shattering Experience," Skeptic Blacksheep, May 10, 2009, http://theskepticblacksheep.wordpress.com/2009/05/10/the-end-of-the-world-part-1-polar-shift-an-earth-shattering-experience/ (January 3, 2011).

36 Oceanside Photo and Telescope, "Jupiter Effect," OPT, 2008, http://www.optcorp.com/edu/articledetailedu.aspx?Aid=2243 (January 3, 2011).

48 William K. Hartmann, *Moons and Planets* (Belmont, CA: Wadsworth, 1999), 149.

90 New Mexico Department of Cultural Affairs, "International Space Hall of Fame," New Mexico Museum of Space History, 2005–2011, http://www.nmspacemuseum.org/halloffame/detail.php?Id=27 (January 3, 2011).

SELECTED BIBLIOGRAPHY

Asimov, Isaac. *A Choice of Catastrophes*. New York: Ballantine Books, 1981.

Barry, John M. *The Great Influenza*. New York: Penguin Books, 2005.

Deconinck, Tony. "2012: Psychology of the Apocalypse (Part 2)." *AolNews*, June 11, 2010. http://www.aolnews.com/weird-news/article/2012-psychology-of-the-apocalypse-part-2/19502324 (August 10, 2010).

Dixon, Dougal. *After Man*. New York: St. Martin's Griffin, 1998.

Faure, Gunter, and Teresa Mensing. *Introduction to Planetary Science*. Dordrecht, Netherlands: Springer Verlag, 2007.

Gardner, Martin. *Fads and Fallacies in the Name of Science*. New York: Dover, 1957.

Grant, John. *Bogus Science*. London: Facts, Figures & Fun, 2009.

Hartmann, William K. *Astronomy: The Cosmic Journey*. Belmont, CA: Wadsworth Publishing Co., 1985.

———. *The History of Earth*. New York: Workman Publishing Co., 1991.

Hartmann, William K., and Ron Miller. *Cycles of Fire*. New York: Workman Publishing Co., 1987.

Heiser, Mike. "Archive for the 'Sitchin' Category." PaleoBabble. N.d. http://michaelsheiser.com/PaleoBabble/category/ancientastronauts/sitchin/ (August 10, 2010).

Heuer, Kenneth. *The End of the World*. New York: Rinehart & Co., 1953.

Impey, Chris. *How It Ends: From You to the Universe*. New York: W. W. Norton, 2010.

Moore, Patrick. *The Universe for the Beginner*. Cambridge: Cambridge University Press, 1992.

National Weather Service. "Space Weather Prediction Center." National Oceanic and Atmospheric Administration. August 24, 2007. http://www .swpc.noaa.gov/Education/index.html (August 10, 2010).

Plait, Phil. "The Planet X Saga: The Scientific Arguments in a Nutshell." Bad Astronomy. 2008. http://www.badastronomy.com/bad/misc/planetx/ nutshell.html (August 10, 2010).

Rowe, David L. *God's Strange Work: William Miller and the End of the World*. Grand Rapids: William B. Eerdmans Publishing Company, 2008.

Verschuur, Gerrit L. *Impact! The Threat of Comets and Asteroids*. New York: Oxford University Press, 1997.

Ward, Peter. *Future Evolution*. New York: W. H. Freeman, 2001.

FURTHER READING, FILMS, AND WEBSITES

NONFICTION

Amsel, Sheri. *365 Ways to Live Green for Kids*. Avon, MA: Adams Media, 2008.
Everyone can pitch in to fight global warming. In this book for young readers, Amsel offers Earth-saving activities for every day of the year.

Andryszewski, Tricia. *Mass Extinction*. Minneapolis: Twenty First Century Books, 2008. Air and water pollution, global warming, and the encroachment of humans on their habitat are causing the deaths of thousands of plant and animal species. The author examines the crisis and what might be done to stop it.

Asimov, Isaac. *Death from Space: What Killed the Dinosaurs?* Milwaukee: Gareth Stevens Publishing, 1994.
Scientists believe that an asteroid crashed into Earth 65 million years ago. The resulting explosion sent tons of dust and smoke into the atmosphere, blotting out the Sun. Without sunlight, plants and animals died. Dinosaurs were among the species wiped out. In this book, famous science writer Isaac Asimov tells the story.

Beyer, Mark. *Nuclear Weapons and the Cold War*. New York: Rosen Publishing Group, 2004.
 A nuclear war would likely kill every living thing on Earth. The threat of nuclear conflict was very real during the Cold War between the United States and the Soviet Union—and the threat is still with us.

Chalmers, Catherine. *Earth's Growing Population*. Chicago: Heinemann Library, 2009.
 Earth is already overcrowded. What will happen later in the century, when billions more people live on Earth? This book examines the impending crisis.

Doeden, Matt. *Human Travel to the Moon and Mars: Waste of Money or Next Frontier?* Minneapolis: Twenty-First Century Books, 2012.
 Scientists have been talking about setting up space colonies for decades. Has the time come for humans to colonize Mars or the Moon? This book examines the pros and cons.

Fleischer, Paul. *The Big Bang*. Minneapolis: Twenty-First Century Books, 2005.
 How did the universe begin? Most scientists think it began with a big bang—with everything exploding out from a central point. Will the universe keep expanding forever until we reach the big chill? This book examines the big bang theory.

Goldsmith, Connie. *Influenza: The Next Pandemic?* Minneapolis: Twenty-First Century Books, 2006.
 Goldsmith, a nurse and medical writer, describes historical pandemics, including the influenza pandemic of 1918–1919. She examines the flu virus and discusses whether another flu pandemic might strike the human population.

———. *Superbugs Strike Back: When Antibiotics Fail*. Minneapolis: Twenty-First Century Books, 2006.
 What happens when antibiotics are no longer effective against bacteria? Goldsmith examines the frightening possibilities.

Hansen, Rosanna. *Seven Wonders of the Sun and Other Stars*. Minneapolis: Twenty-First Century Books, 2011.
 Hansen explains how stormy weather on the Sun can cause problems for people on Earth. She also looks beyond the Sun to other stars in the universe.

Jefferis, David. *Black Holes: And Other Bizarre Space Objects*. New York: Crabtree Publishing Company, 2006.
 It's unlikely, but if Earth were ever to encounter a black hole, it would truly be the end of the world. This book explores black holes and other space phenomena, including killer gamma-ray bursts.

Koppes, Steven. *Killer Rocks from Outer Space*. Minneapolis: Twenty-First Century Books. 2003.
What would happen if an asteroid struck Earth? It's happened before—and if it happened again, the results could be devastating.

Miller, Ron. *The Sun*. Minneapolis: Twenty-First Century Books, 2002.
This book tells the story of our star, the Sun, from its birth to its inevitable death.

Nardo, Don. *Biological Warfare*. Detroit: Lucent Books, 2006.
Whether used by a regular army or a terrorist group, biological weapons would do great devastation. This title examines the history—and terrifying future—of biological warfare.

Newman, Kim. *Apocalypse Movies*. New York: St. Martin's Press, 2000.
This title gives a history of the end of the world as depicted in motion pictures.

Tanaka, Shelley. *Climate Change*. Toronto: Groundwood Books, 2007.
This book examines many aspects of global warming, including what causes it and what can be done about it.

Woods, Mary B., and Michael Woods. *Earthquakes*. Minneapolis: Twenty-First Century Books, 2007.
Illustrated with diagrams, maps, and full-color photographs, this book explains what happens—both above- and belowground—when an earthquake strikes.

FICTION

Brin, David. *The Postman*. Toronto: Bantam Books, 1985.
Communication has broken down following a global war, and a lone man tries to hold civilization together by acting as a messenger. The novel was made into a movie in 1997.

Collins, Suzanne. *The Hunger Games*. New York: Scholastic Press, 2008.
This book for young adult readers is set in the future, when the United States has collapsed due to drought, fire, famine, and war. Society has resorted to televised brutality. This first book in a trilogy was followed by *Catching Fire* and *Mockingjay*.

Heinlein, Robert A. *Farnham's Freehold*. Riverdale, NY: Baen, 1964.
A family tries to survive after most of the world is destroyed by a nuclear war.

Kunstler, James Howard. *World Made by Hand*. New York: Atlantic Monthly Press, 2008.
After oil wells run dry, people can no longer use oil for fuel. The economy collapses, and society begins to break down. Set in the United States in the not-too-distant future, Kunstler's novel shows how one man tries to cope with the crisis.

Miller, Walter M. *A Canticle for Leibowitz*. Philadelphia: Lippincott, 1960.
Miller's acclaimed novel deals with the struggle to preserve civilization following a worldwide nuclear war.

O'Brien, Robert C. *Z for Zachariah*. New York: Simon Pulse, 2007.
In this novel for young readers, Ann Burden thinks she is alone in the world after a nuclear war. But it turns out she's not the only one left.

Pfeffer, Susan Beth. *Life as We Knew It*. New York: Graphia, 2008.
This young adult novel includes an asteroid strike, violent earthquakes, killer tsunamis, disease outbreaks, and the deaths of millions of people. Teenage Miranda must struggle to survive in this horrifying new world.

FILMS

The Book of Eli. DVD. Los Angeles: Warner Brothers, 2010.
Set in postapocalyptic America, *The Book of Eli* features superstar Denzel Washington as a drifter with a sacred book. He survives by hunting small animals and foraging through the wreckage of former homes and towns. His book holds the secret to saving humanity.

Children of Men. DVD. Los Angeles: Universal Pictures, 2006.
In this film, set in the near future, a mysterious disease prevents women from becoming pregnant. The human race must face the possibility of dying out. Clive Owen, Michael Caine, and Julianne Moore play leading roles.

The Day after Tomorrow. DVD. Los Angeles: Twentieth Century Fox, 2004.
In this exciting and thought-provoking movie, climate change has brought about a new ice age, encasing the northern half of Earth in ice. Dennis Quaid and Jake Gyllenhaal play a father and a son in a struggle for survival.

Deep Impact. DVD. Hollywood, CA: Paramount Pictures, 1998.
A comet is on a collision course with Earth. What can humanity do to save itself? Morgan Freeman plays the president of the United States, with other leading roles played by Robert Duvall, Téa Leoni, John Favreau, Blair Underwood, and Elijah Wood.

Dr. Strangelove. DVD. Culver City, CA: Columbia Pictures Corporation, 1964.
In this black comedy, an insane military officer starts a nuclear war. Legendary actors Peter Sellers, George C. Scott, Sterling Hayden, and James Earl Jones are among the stars.

The Road. DVD. New York: Dimension Films, 2009.
In this grim film, based on a novel by Cormac McCarthy, a father and a son struggle to survive in postapocalyptic America. Meanwhile, society has decayed into lawlessness, and bands of cannibals stalk the landscape. The film stars big-name actors Viggo Mortensen, Robert Duvall, and Guy Pearce.

WEBSITES

Asteroid
http://www.pbs.org/wgbh/nova/space/asteroid.html
This website, a companion to the *Nova* television program of the same name, examines the possibility of an asteroid striking Earth. The site includes interviews with scientists and an interactive "catastrophe calculator."

Doomsday Clock
http://www.thebulletin.org/content/doomsday-clock/overview
This Web page from the *Bulletin of the Atomic Scientists* examines three threats that might wipe out humanity: nuclear war, climate change, and biological technology.

Global Warming
http://topics.nytimes.com/top/news/science/topics/globalwarming/index.html
This page from the *New York Times* explains global warming and includes dozens of in-depth articles on the topic. It also includes maps, illustrations, and links to additional information.

The Great 2012 Doomsday Scare
http://www.nasa.gov/topics/earth/features/2012-guest.html
On this Web page, astronomers answer questions about 2012 end-of-the-world predictions, explaining how none of them are based in fact.

Influenza 1918
http://www.pbs.org/wgbh/americanexperience/films/influenza/
The flu pandemic of 1918 killed more people than World War I. This website, a companion to the *American Experience* television program of the same name, examines the pandemic through photographs, interviews, and other primary documentation.

The Millennium and End-of-the-World-as-We-Know-It Prophecies
http://www.religioustolerance.org/end_wrld.htm
This site offers a comprehensive list of end-of-the-world predictions in religion and myth.

Planet X
http://www.badastronomy.com/bad/misc/planetx/
An astronomer looks at the myth surrounding "Planet X," which some say will bring about the end of the world in 2012.

2012Hoax
http://www.2012hoax.org
This website not only debunks 2012 end-of-the-world predictions, but it also examines pseudoscientific and other end-of-the-world myths.

INDEX

ABOUT THE AUTHOR

Hugo Award–winning author and illustrator Ron Miller specializes in books about science. Among his many titles, he has written *The Elements: What You Really Want to Know* and *Special Effects: An Introduction to Movie Magic*. His favorite subjects are space and astronomy. A postage stamp he created is currently on board a spaceship headed for Pluto. His original paintings can be found in collections all over the world. Miller lives in Virginia.

PHOTO ACKNOWLEDGMENTS

The images in this book are used with the permission of: © Ron Miller, pp. 1 (and all star backgrounds), 26-27, 33, 37, 46-47, 53, 54, 56, 63, 66 (bottom), 68–69, 87, 88–89, 92, 94–95, 96–97, 98, 98–99, 101, 104; NASA/JSC, pp. 4–5, 42, 45; © Mitchell Funk/Photographer's Choice/Getty Images, pp. 6–7; © Arni Magnusson Institute, Reykjavik, Iceland/The Bridgeman Art Library, p. 8; © The Bridgeman Art Library/Getty Images, p. 10; © Hulton Archive/Getty Images, p. 12; © Mary Evans Picture Library/The Image Works, p. 14; The Art Archive/National Archives, Washington DC, p. 15; Paramount/The Kobal Collection, p. 16; United Artists/The Kobal Collection, p. 17 (top); Columbia/The Kobal Collection, p. 17 (bottom); Hawk Film Prod/Columbia/The Kobal Collection, p. 18; Dreamworks/Paramount/The Kobal Collection, pp. 18–19; © Sergio Pitamitz/SuperStock, pp. 20–21; © Ron Dahlquist/SuperStock, p. 22; © Jerry Lodriguss/Photo Researchers, Inc., p. 23; © Todd Strand/Independent Picture Service, p. 25; © ps1/picturesbyrob/Alamy, p. 26; © Joe Raedle/Getty Images, pp. 28–29; © Casey & Clancey/Buyenlarge/Archive Photos/Getty Images, p. 31 (top); AP Photo/Doug Pizac, p. 31 (bottom); © BSIP/Photo Researchers, Inc., p. 32; Kyodo via AP Images, p. 34 (top); © Mark A. Johnson/Workbook Stock/Getty Images, p. 34 (bottom); © Roger Harris/Photo Researchers, Inc., p. 38; SOHO (ESA & NASA), pp. 40–41; © age fotostock/SuperStock, p. 43; NASA/GSFC/Gary Rottman (University of Colorado/LASP), p. 44 (top); © Royal Astronomical Society/Photo Researchers, Inc., p. 44 (bottom); © Francois Gohier/Photo Researchers, Inc., p. 47; © Science Source/Photo Researchers, Inc., p. 48; © John R. Foster/Photo Researchers, Inc., pp. 50–51; © G. Butler/Photo Researchers, Inc., p. 50; NASA/MSFC/SEDS/D. Seal/CXC/M. Weiss, p. 52; © Ircrockett/Dreamstime.com, p. 58; NASA/Goddard Space Flight Center Scientific Visualization Studio, p. 60; © The Asahi Shimbun Premium via Getty Images, p. 65; © Kevin Schafer/The Image Bank/Getty Images, p. 66 (top); © Gino Rigucci/Dreamstime.com, p. 67; AP Photo/The Knoxville News Sentinel, Clay Owen, p. 71; © Tokyo Electric Power Company/Jana Press/ZUMA Press, p. 73; © New York Public Library/Photo Researchers, Inc., pp. 74–75; © Justin Sullivan/Getty Images, p. 76; © Andy Crump, TDR, World Health Organization/Photo Researchers, Inc., p. 77; © Greg Wood/AFP/Getty Images, p. 78; The Granger Collection, New York, p. 79; © Chris Kleponis/AFP/Getty Images, p. 80; © Pictorial Parade/Archive Photos/Getty Images, p. 81; AP Photo/APTN, p. 83; AP Photo/Hakon Mosvold Larsen, Pool, p. 84; AP Photo/Str, p. 86; NASA, p. 91 (top); NASA/GRC, p. 91 (middle); NASA Ames Research Center, p. 91 (bottom); © Jon Brenneis/Time & Life Pictures/Getty Images, p. 100; NASA, ESA and the Hubble Heritage Team (STScI/AURA)-ESA/Hubble Collaboration, Acknowledgement: B. Whitmore (Space Telescope Science Institute), pp. 102-103; © Jewel Samad/AFP/Getty Images, p. 107 (top); © Suzanne Laird/The Image Bank/Getty Images, p. 107 (bottom).

Front cover: © Ron Miller.